MOMENTS OF PEACE
from the Bible

_____

PRESENTED TO

_____

PRESENTED BY

_____

DATE

MOMENTS
of
PEACE
from the
PSALMS

*Reflections on God's Gifts of
Encouragement, Love, and Power*

MOMENTS
of
PEACE
from the
PSALMS

BETHANYHOUSE
MINNEAPOLIS, MINNESOTA

Moments of Peace From the Psalms
Copyright © 2007 by GRQ, Inc.

Published by Bethany House Publishers
11400 Hampshire Avenue South
Bloomington, Minnesota 55438

Bethany House Publishers is a division of Baker Publishing Group, Grand Rapids, Michigan.

Scripture quotations noted AMP are from The Amplified Bible, Old Testament. Copyright © 1965, 1987 by The Zondervan Corporation. The Amplified New Testament, copyright © 1954, 1958, 1987 by The Lockman Foundation. Used by permission.

Scripture quotations noted CEV are taken from THE CONTEMPORARY ENGLISH VERSION. Copyright © 1991 by the American Bible Society. Used by permission.

Scripture quotations noted ESV are from The Holy Bible, English Standard Version, copyright © 2001 by Crossway Bibles, a division of Good News Publishers. Used by permission. All rights reserved.

Scripture quotations noted GOD'S WORD are from *God's Word*, a copyrighted work of God's Word to the Nations Bible Society. Copyright © 1995 by God's Word to the Nations Bible Society. Used by permission. All rights reserved.

Scripture quotations noted GNT are from the Good News Translation, Second Edition, copyright © 1992 by American Bible Society. Used by permission. All rights reserved.

Scripture quotations noted HCSB have been taken from the Holman Christian Standard Bible®, Copyright © 1999, 2000, 2002, 2003 by Holman Bible Publishers. Used by permission. Holman Christian Standard Bible®, Holman CSB® and HCSB® are federally registered trademarks of Holman Bible Publishers.

Scripture quotations noted MSG are taken from *THE MESSAGE: The New Testament, Psalms and Proverbs.* Copyright © 1993, 1994, 1995 by Eugene H. Peterson. All rights reserved.

Scripture quotations noted NASB are taken from the NEW AMERICAN STANDARD BIBLE® Copyright © 1960, 1962, 1963–1968, 1971, 1973–1975, 1977, 1995 by the Lockman Foundation. Used by permission.

Scripture quotations noted NCV are from The Holy Bible, New Century Version, copyright © 1987, 1988, 1991 by Word Publishing, a division of Thomas Nelson, Inc. All rights reserved. Used by permission.

Scripture quotations noted NIV are taken from the *Holy Bible: New International Version* (North American Edition)®. Copyright © 1973–1978, 1984, by the International Bible Society. Used by permission of Zondervan. All rights reserved.

Scripture quotations noted NKJV are taken from THE NEW KING JAMES VERSION. Copyright © 1979, 1980, 1982, Thomas Nelson, Inc., Publishers.

Scripture quotation noted NLT are taken from the *Holy Bible,* New Living Translation, copyright © 1996. Used by permission of Tyndale House Publishers, Inc., Wheaton, Illinois 60189. All rights reserved.

All rights reserved. No part of this publication may be reproduced, stored in a retrieval system, or transmitted in any form or by any means—electronic, mechanical, photocopying, recording, or any other—without the prior written permission of the publisher. The only exception is brief quotations in printed reviews.

ISBN 978-0-7642-0420-3

Editor: Lila Empson
Associate Editor: Natasha Sperling
Writer: Jennifer B. Rosania
Design: Whisner Design Group

Printed in China. All rights reserved under International Copyright Law. Contents and/or cover may not be reproduced in whole or in part in any form without the express written consent of the publisher.

08 09 10   8 7 6 5 4

Worship God in adoring embrace,
celebrate in trembling awe.
Psalm 2:11 MSG

CONTENTS

INTRODUCTION

Hello, friend. Thank you for spending time with God!

Throughout the ages, the book of Psalms has been an inspiration to countless people. Not only does it hold some of the most beautiful verses ever written about the joys and sorrows of the human heart, but it also brings you to the very throne of heaven with how it describes your loving God.

Originally a worship book for the people of Israel, Psalms was compiled during a time period of more than a thousand years—from the time of the Exodus from Egypt until after the Babylonian captivity. Seventy-three of the psalms were composed by King David; however, Moses, Solomon, Asaph, and possibly even King Hezekiah also contributed to this exquisite book of hymns, prayers, and poetry. Their insight is recorded there to encourage you and bring you closer to God.

Moments of Peace From the Psalms has been written with you in mind—connecting the daily struggles you face with the profound wisdom of God's Word. You will discover the intimate relationship God wants to have with you, and how he can be your Defender, Provider, Healer, and King no matter what you face.

Friend, God is waiting to fill you with joy and comfort you with his presence during these moments of peace each day. So read the inspirational verses, pray, worship God, and enjoy your journey through the psalms. May your time with God completely bless your soul.

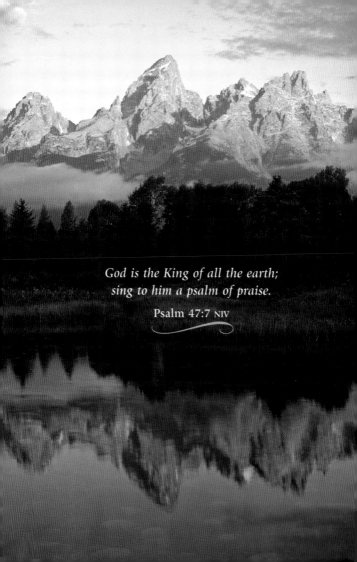

God is the King of all the earth;
sing to him a psalm of praise.

Psalm 47:7 NIV

Seeking God's Love

None of the good promises the LORD had made to the house of Israel failed. Everything was fulfilled.

JOSHUA 21:45 MSG

DEEP ROOTS

They are strong, like a tree planted by a river.
The tree produces fruit in season, and its leaves
don't die. Everything they do will succeed.
PSALM 1:3 NCV

Looking for peace in the Psalms is not a random choice on your part. There's a reason you've come  here. Perhaps you're seeking understanding in a difficult situation. Or maybe you don't know where else to turn. Either way, you're looking in the right place—the only place peace can be found: in God. You'll always find God in his Word.

Like river waters nourishing a tree's roots, when you drink in God's Word, it goes deep into your heart and makes you strong. God's nurturing truth gives you the courage and wisdom for whatever you're facing.

So seek him—allow his Word to take root deep in your heart. You'll be sure to find the peace you're looking for.

God, I know that I haven't come here by chance.
Thank you that the Psalms will strengthen my heart
and nourish my soul. AMEN.

*Delight in doing everything the LORD wants;
day and night . . . think about his law.*

PSALM 1:2 NLT

SURRENDERING TO SENSE

Worship God in adoring embrace,
celebrate in trembling awe.
PSALM 2:11 MSG

Sometimes no matter how hard you try, you cannot understand what is happening to you. The more details you discover, the more confused you become.

 None of the information you are receiving fits together, and you feel as if your mind just can't wrap itself around the situation.

Yet there is One who is great enough to make sense of your circumstances—and wise enough to know what you should do.

When you worship God, focusing on his almighty power and trembling in awe of his wisdom, you realize that there is nothing too big for him to handle. You find peace by focusing on him and surrendering the situation to his care.

God, I come into your presence in worship, adoration,
and surrender. You are truly wise and make
sense of all that concerns me. AMEN.

*Blessed are all those who
put their trust in Him.*

PSALMS 2:12 NKJV

AN IMPENETRABLE DEFENSE

You, O LORD, are a shield for me, my glory and the One who lifts up my head.
PSALM 3:3 NKJV

King David always had plenty of enemies. However, this time, his adversary represented the greatest betrayal, knew David's most profound weak-

nesses, and pierced the deepest part of his heart. This time, the enemy was David's own son Absalom.

Are you facing a problem that's a lose-lose situation no matter how you look at it? You aren't sure whom to trust, and you're heartbroken about the way you've been betrayed? It's difficult to know what to do.

You can always do as David did—count on God as your impenetrable defense, who not only protects your body but guards your heart.

Today don't despair. Rather, trust God to shield you in this situation.

Lord, I know that you can turn this lose-lose situation into a victory. Thank you for being my merciful defender. I trust you. AMEN.

Real help comes from GOD. *Your blessing clothes your people!*

PSALM 3:8 MSG

EVER LISTENING

The Lord will hear when I call to Him.
Psalm 4:3 hcsb

In the silence of the night when your household lies quietly resting, sometimes difficult thoughts will prevail in your mind. Perhaps you've been careful  not to voice your concerns with others because you didn't want to worry them. But in that desolate moment you are alone with your struggles, and you wish someone could share them and comfort you.

God hears you. He is with you, with his ear always bent toward you, waiting for you to invite him into your situation.

You don't have to go on feeling alone. Call out to him and tell him your concerns. Let him comfort you. He's always ready to listen.

God, thank you for your comforting presence in my loneliest hours and for always hearing my prayers. Truly, you are good and loving. Amen.

In peace I will both lie down and sleep, for You, Lord, alone make me dwell in safety and confident trust.

PSALM 4:8 AMP

PREPARED FOR HIS PRESENCE

*By Your abundant lovingkindness I will
enter Your house, at Your holy temple
I will bow in reverence for You.*
PSALM 5:7 NASB

When traveling to another nation, diplomats, businessmen, and missionaries often must engage in extensive study of the culture they're visiting. The kiss  on the cheek that is common in Venezuela would be impolite in Singapore, where the head is considered sacred. Consequently, travelers must train themselves to show respect to the people they're meeting.

The wonderful thing about God is that he himself prepares you to meet with him. He instructs you concerning the habits that please him and cleanses you from those that don't.

Whatever is needed for you to come into God's presence, he provides it. Therefore, don't be shy. He loves you unconditionally, so enjoy his company.

*God, thank you that I don't have to be nervous in
your presence. You want the real me, and that makes
me love you even more. AMEN.*

*In the morning, O LORD, you
hear my voice; in the morning
I lay my requests before you
and wait in expectation.*

PSALM 5:3 NIV

A SURE RESCUE

O Lord, deliver my life; save me for the sake
of Your steadfast love and mercy.
PSALM 6:4 AMP

Perhaps you've opened this devotional today with some important issue pressing on your mind that consumes your energy and creativity. Maybe you've come here wondering two things.

First: Can God help me? Yes, the almighty God who created the universe is certainly able to handle your situation.

Second: Will God help me? This question goes to God's love for you—especially if you've messed up in some way. Yet the answer is yes! His love for you is unconditional, which means he'll surely rescue you.

Today rest in the confidence that God can and will work in your situation. Though it may not be in the way you expect, he'll definitely come to your aid.

God, thank you for loving me unconditionally and help-
ing me. I entrust this situation to you, knowing that
your power will transform my circumstances for good.
AMEN.

The LORD has heard my plea for help;
the LORD accepts my prayer.

PSALM 6:9 HCSB

THE FAIR JUDGE

Awake, my God; decree justice.
PSALM 7:6 NIV

In King Saul's court, many people were jealous that David would succeed Saul as ruler of Israel. So they made trouble for David—telling Saul that

David wanted to kill him. This, of course, was a lie. So David cried out to God to reveal the truth.

When people concoct falsehoods about you, sometimes the worst part is that you can't defend yourself. Their cruel fabrications endanger your reputation, relationships, and even your future.

Yet you don't have to avenge yourself—God will come to your defense as he did for David. Today be patient and honor God in everything you do. Soon enough, you'll see his justice done and your false accusers exposed.

Thank you, Lord, for seeing the truth and making it known. It may take some time, but you're a fair Judge, and justice will be done. AMEN.

*Judge me and show that I am honest
and innocent. You know every heart
and mind, and you always do right.
Now make violent people stop, but
protect all of us who obey you.*

PSALM 7:8–9 CEV

GOD OF THE GLORIOUS HEAVENS

O LORD, our Lord, your greatness is seen in all the world! Your praise reaches up to the heavens.
PSALM 8:1 GNT

Even with all of the technology available to us, we can't count all the stars in the universe or estimate the light and energy that are generated through

them. Still, knowing that the sun converts more than 250 million tons of matter into illumination and heat every minute gives us a clue concerning the immensity of what's occurring.

Yet even the centillions of stars that exist together pale in comparison to the splendor of God. And he wants to show his glory to others through you.

So whenever you feel insignificant, consider the radiant heavenly bodies. Then remember that as his best creation, God is shining even more brightly in you.

God, truly you are more brilliant and beautiful than all the stars in the universe! May my life reflect your glory and draw others to you. AMEN.

I see the moon and stars, which you created. But why are people important to you? Why do you take care of human beings? You . . . crowned them with glory and honor.

PSALM 8:3–5 NCV

HIS NAME IS TRUSTWORTHY

*Those who know your name put their trust
in you, for you, O LORD, have not
forsaken those who seek you.*
PSALM 9:10 ESV

You may be wondering what it means when you're
reading the Bible and you see the word LORD in all
capitals. This was the way translators signified that

God's name had been used
in the original text.

In Hebrew, God's name is
transliterated Yahweh, which
means "I AM." He is the living God, who is as faithful
and loving today as he was
to all generations before—and as he'll continue to be
for all eternity. That is why you can trust God, because
he is consistently and unchangingly honorable.

The psalmists saw God's faithfulness proven daily,
and you can as well. Call upon his name. You'll certainly find that he's completely trustworthy.

*My God, the great I AM, I thank you for being utterly
dependable and reliable, faithful and trustworthy.
May your name always be praised. AMEN.*

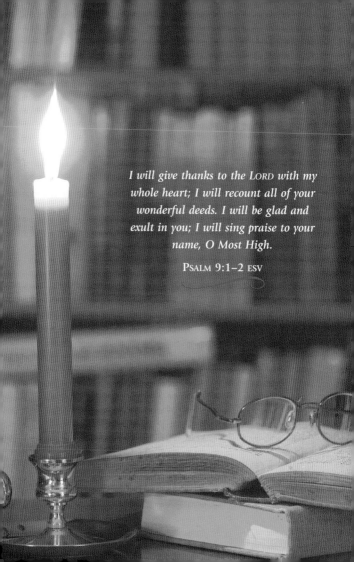

I will give thanks to the Lord with my whole heart; I will recount all of your wonderful deeds. I will be glad and exult in you; I will sing praise to your name, O Most High.

PSALM 9:1–2 ESV

WHO QUALIFIES?

LORD, you know the hopes of the helpless. Surely you will listen to their cries and comfort them.
PSALM 10:17 NLT

When the giant Goliath challenged Israel to send out its mightiest warrior for a duel, no one imagined that it would be David who'd do the job. The youngest,

weakest, and least impressive of his brothers, David was a mere shepherd boy—completely unskilled in the issues of war. Nonetheless, God was with him, and Goliath was defeated.

You may believe that only the wealthy, strong, or brave qualify for God's help. However, God aids whoever calls upon him, honors him, and entrusts themselves to his care.

No matter what giant problem you face today, trust God to make you victorious. Commit to doing his will, and watch every obstacle crumble before you.

God, thank you that your only requirement for me is that I be willing to obey you. I praise you that when I'm weak, you're strong. AMEN.

You take notice of trouble and suffering and are always ready to help. The helpless commit themselves to you; you have always helped the needy.

<small>Psalm 10:14 GNT</small>

TRUE STABILITY

The Lord is in his holy temple; the Lord is on his heavenly throne.
PSALM 11:4 NIV

Your life can change in an instant—you get a bad doctor's report or are the victim of a crime; you lose a job or, worse, a loved one. In that horrible moment

you experience something that leaves you reeling in pain and confusion. Perhaps your sense of stability is seriously damaged, and nothing provides any security or peace.

When your world is shaken, turn to the One who is completely unwavering. No matter what's happened to you, God is still on the throne, and he's able to help and comfort you. So don't look any further—embrace the only security that will never fail. God will surely keep you stable and strong. Trust him.

Lord, I'm so glad that no matter what happens, you are my stability and strength. Your love gives me hope when everything else fails. AMEN.

The LORD always does right and
wants justice done. Everyone who
does right will see his face.

PSALM 11:7 CEV

WORDS

The words of the LORD are pure words, like
silver tried in a furnace of earth,
purified seven times.
PSALM 12:6 NKJV

It's often been said that words cannot injure like a rock or a stick could, but the truth is that sometimes they wound you in a manner that's far more danger-ous. While physical abrasions heal, abrasions made by words can pierce the heart and fester. Years after you've forgotten they were said, abrasive words can cripple you in ways you don't even realize.

Yet God knows they're there, and he looks upon you with compassion. He sends his Word to heal you—to root out the wounding words and restore you.

Other people may hurt you with their words, but God never will. Today trust him and allow his Word to do its uplifting work.

Heal me, Lord, from the wounding words of others. I
thank you that your Word is pure, powerful, and
always trustworthy. AMEN.

The LORD replies, "I have seen violence
done to the helpless, and I have heard
the groans of the poor. Now I will
rise up to rescue them, as they
have longed for me to do."

PSALM 12:5–6 NLT

WAITING FOR AN ANSWER

Please listen, LORD God, and answer my
prayers. Make my eyes sparkle again.
PSALM 13:3 CEV

As you know, there are consequences to waiting. When you ask God about something important and he doesn't answer right away, you'll not only  struggle with your own doubts, but you may have to address the questions of others. They will want to know what your course of action will be and why you're allowing opportunities to pass by. You may not have any answers.

In those times, it'll be difficult to keep waiting—but do it anyway. Allowing God to answer will strengthen your faith. Be patient, friend. God will undoubtedly answer you in a way that will bring that sparkle back to your eyes. Count on it.

Lord, waiting is extremely difficult, but I will trust
you. I know that you will never let me down and that
your promises are sure. AMEN.

I've thrown myself headlong into your arms—
I'm celebrating your rescue. I'm singing at the
top of my lungs, I'm so full of answered prayers.

PSALM 13:5–6 MSG

THE SEEKERS

*From heaven the L*ORD *looks down to see if
anyone is wise enough to search for him.*
PSALM 14:2 CEV

What do you think God is looking for when he
peers down from heaven? Why do you suppose God
would bother to look away from the glorious beauty
of his celestial home?

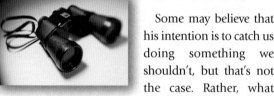

Some may believe that
his intention is to catch us
doing something we
shouldn't, but that's not
the case. Rather, what
God is observing is something very precious to
him—he's watching for people who are looking for
him. He's searching for seekers who know that
there's more to this life than the affairs of this world.

Are you seeking God? Then he's looking down
from heaven at you. And he just loves the fact that
you want to know him.

*God, I want to love you with all my heart. Thank you
for all the ways you make yourself known to me.*
AMEN.

God is with those who obey him.

PSALM 14:5 GNT

All Your Plans

*May he give you the desire of
your heart and make all your
plans succeed.*

PSALM 20:4 NIV

WORTHY OF HIS HOUSE

LORD, who may abide in Your tent?
Who may dwell on Your holy hill?
PSALM 15:1 NASB

Who is fit for heaven? What does it take to be close to God? Psalm 15 says that you must be blameless, virtuous, and truthful, and never speak  badly of others. You must never accept money that comes from taking advantage of others, you must keep your oaths, and you must never do any wrong.

Does this sound unfeasible? In a sense, it's supposed to be. Your failings were meant to show you that it's impossible for anyone to make himself or herself fit for heaven. That's why you must depend on Jesus to make you worthy of his house through his death and resurrection. He makes you completely fit. Believe in him.

Jesus, thank you for preparing me to live in heaven
with you. Thank you for making the impossible
possible for me. AMEN.

*Whoever does these things
will always be secure.*

PSALM 15:5 GNT

BLESSINGS AHEAD

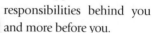

LORD, You are my portion and my cup
[of blessing]; You hold my future.
PSALM 16:5 HCSB

Caught in traffic and feeling the anxiety of the things you have to accomplish today, the only thing ahead seems to be the unblinking red taillights of the car in front of you. You're stopped—stuck—with responsibilities behind you and more before you.

Friend, this situation is frustrating because you cannot see any relief or reward in the future, but don't make the mistake of thinking that things will never change. God is going to bless your hard work and faithfulness.

Go to God for comfort in these wearisome times and draw your strength from him. Be patient and keep watch. Soon enough, the light will turn green on all of your blessings.

God, thank you for holding my future and planning
wonderful blessings ahead. Even though I cannot see
them, I trust that you'll provide them. AMEN.

I keep the LORD in mind always.
Because He is at my right hand,
I will not be shaken.

PSALM 16:8 HCSB

THE PATH OF LIFE

You will show me the way of life, granting me the joy of your presence and the pleasures of living with you forever.
PSALM 16:11 NLT

There's a big difference between those who make promises and those who actually keep them. There are many who guarantee that their product or belief  system will bring you happiness in this life. Unfortunately, their solutions are only temporary. They disregard that your nature is eternal and fail to give you real contentment.

But God not only gives you joy in this life, he's actively preparing you for eternity. You can trust him to show you the truly wonderful path of your future.

God keeps his promises forever and knows what will bring real peace and joy to your soul. So follow him. No doubt you'll find the way lined with unending blessings.

God, I confess that I've sought temporary fixes for the hunger of my soul. Thank you for showing me the joyous path of everlasting life. AMEN.

My heart is glad and my glory rejoices;
my flesh also will dwell securely. For
You will not abandon my soul.

PSALM 16:9–10 NASB

EXONERATED

May my vindication come from you;
may your eyes see what is right.
PSALM 17:2 NIV

Whether they're being intentionally destructive or just foolish, some people can make terrible decisions. Unfortunately, their choices can seriously  harm your character, and you know that if you continue to associate with them, you'll be dishonoring God.

When you're in such a situation, your only acceptable course of action will be to walk away. Of course, that decision will involve consequences that frighten you, and you'll wonder if the opposition you'll face is worth it.

Friend, just remember that your first responsibility is to God. If he shows you that leaving is the right thing to do, you have no reason to fear. God will make the justice of your choice known in due time.

God, I'm scared, but I want to honor you. Please
protect me and vindicate me. Please show me
what I should do. AMEN.

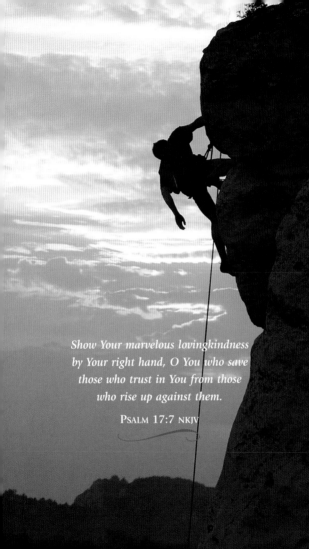

Show Your marvelous lovingkindness
by Your right hand, O You who save
those who trust in You from those
who rise up against them.

PSALM 17:7 NKJV

HEMMED IN, SET FREE

He brought me out to a wide-open place;
He rescued me because He delighted in me.
PSALM 18:19 HCSB

Some days you'll wonder how you got to where you are—completely entangled in the strong cords of duty and difficulty. You've been following God,

and you can't understand why he'd allow the weight of your burdens to crush you in such a way. You feel that if another problem comes to you, you'll break.

Don't despair, friend. God hemmed you in for a reason. He's bringing you into a place of freedom, but first he must teach you to trust him for today.

So stop worrying about the future and focus on honoring God with the task that's in front of you. He loves you and will set you free; only trust him.

God, I thank you for teaching me to trust
you during this difficult time. Help me to
honor you in all that I do. AMEN.

The L<small>ORD</small> rewarded me according to my righteousness; according to the cleanness of my hands He has recompensed me.

P<small>SALM</small> 18:20 NKJV

TAKING YOU HIGHER UP

He makes me like a deer that does not stumble; he helps me stand on the steep mountains.

PSALM 18:33 NCV

There are certain things that you can learn only by doing them. No amount of explanation of geological formations can prepare a young deer or goat for getting up to the apex of a mountain. Rather, the deer or goat must strengthen its muscles by actually climbing.

Likewise, your faith can only grow in the midst of the doubts and unknowns of your circumstances. You exercise your trust in God, and he strengthens your spiritual muscles so that you can reach higher and achieve more with him.

When you follow God, life is a wonderful adventure. So get ready for the climb, friend. The view is truly worth it.

God, thank you for training me for the heights through my circumstances. I know that with you, I'll achieve all I've been created for. AMEN.

*You have also given me the shield of
Your salvation, and Your right
hand upholds me; and Your
gentleness makes me great.*

PSALM 18:35 NASB

HUMBLY BEFORE HIM

*Let the words of my mouth and the meditation
of my heart be acceptable in Your sight,
O LORD, my strength and my Redeemer.*
PSALM 19:14 NKJV

Do you ever feel uncomfortable when talking to
God? Does communicating with him intimidate

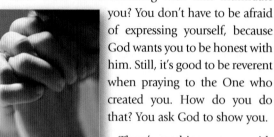

you? You don't have to be afraid
of expressing yourself, because
God wants you to be honest with
him. Still, it's good to be reverent
when praying to the One who
created you. How do you do
that? You ask God to show you.

There's nothing wrong with
asking God to help you honor
his majesty. In fact, he loves it when you want to
learn from him.

So today seek his wisdom and instruction—he's
certainly able to show you what an honest, worshipful, humble heart looks like. Don't be afraid. God
delights in teaching you how to have a deeper
relationship with him.

*God, I want my words and thoughts to be acceptable
to you. Please teach me how to honor you
and love you more. AMEN.*

The statutes of the LORD are trustworthy, making wise the simple. The precepts of the LORD are right, giving joy to the heart.

PSALM 19:7–8 NIV

A PRAYER FOR YOU

*May he give you the desire of your heart and
make all your plans succeed.*
PSALM 20:4 NIV

Friend, today these words rise up to God on your
behalf. As you go, may he answer your prayers and
protect you from trouble. May he make you aware of

the many amazing ways
he's working around you
and empowering you—
giving you wisdom and
creativity—for all of your
tasks.

May God remember all
the ways you've served him
faithfully. May He give you the desire of your heart
and bring success to all your plans.

Today these words rise up to God that you would
trust him and commit to obeying him. May all who
know you praise God for the magnificent victories
he gives you and his unending love for you. Amen.

*God, thank you for this prayer today, and for giving
me success. May my life bring you much praise, for
you are truly worthy. AMEN.*

We will shout for joy over your victory
and celebrate your triumph by
praising our God. May the LORD
answer all your requests.

PSALM 20:5 GNT

AUTHENTIC POWER

*Some trust in their war chariots and others in
their horses, but we trust in the power
of the LORD our God.*
PSALM 20:7 GNT

Imagine being a soldier on the field of battle. The
enemy armies of Ammon and Aram are thundering
toward you with armaments of war that you've only

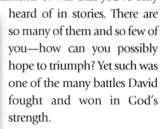

heard of in stories. There are
so many of them and so few of
you—how can you possibly
hope to triumph? Yet such was
one of the many battles David
fought and won in God's
strength.

Do you face a battle today
in which the resources of your adversary far outpace
your own? Do not fear—God is with you. Their com-
bat assets may create the illusion of power, but nothing can overcome the mighty strength of the Lord.
Trust him for your victory.

*God, yours is the only authentic power, so I have
nothing to fear. Thank you for bringing me
victory in this situation. AMEN.*

I know that the Lord saves His anointed; He will answer him from His holy heaven with the saving strength of His right hand.

PSALM 20:6 AMP

VICTORY IS HIS GOAL

How the king rejoices in your strength, O LORD!
He shouts with joy because of your victory.
PSALM 21:1 NLT

It's not necessary to understand why God leads you in a certain way—it's only necessary to obey him. Even when he appears to direct you away from your goal, trust him.

This may not seem logical, but there are factors that affect your situation that you simply cannot see. Fortunately, God is well aware of those influences, and he sees the path ahead of you. He knows exactly what you will need to succeed.

So trust him and obey his instruction. Soon enough, all of his seemingly illogical directions will reveal the straightest path to your triumph. And you'll find that your victory was his goal the whole time.

God, thank you for leading me. I trust you even when I don't understand your directions. Thank you that with you, the victory is assured. AMEN.

You have given him his heart's desire and have not withheld the request of his lips.

PSALM 21:2 AMP

ENDING IN PRAISE

In the midst of the congregation will I praise
You. You who fear (revere and worship)
the Lord, praise Him!
PSALM 22:22–23 AMP

Psalm 22 was written about one thousand years
before Jesus was born, but it forecasts many things
that happened during his trial
and crucifixion. It may appear
strange that a psalm that envi-
sions such a difficult event
would contain such praise as
you find in vv. 22–23. Yet it
movingly depicts the hopeful-
ness you can have in your most
difficult situations.

Just as Jesus did not stay in the grave but was glo-
riously resurrected, the dreams that have died for
you will come to life again. That's why you can
praise in the midst of your troubles. Because when
you trust in Jesus, death isn't final. Rather, joy and
life are your ultimate destination.

God, thank you that I can end in praise because of
your wondrous work in my life. To you be all
honor and glory. AMEN.

Our ancestors trusted you, and you rescued them. When they cried out for help, you saved them, and you did not let them down when they depended on you.

PSALM 22:4–5 CEV

THE SHEPHERD PROVIDES

The LORD is my shepherd;
I have everything I need.
PSALM 23:1 NCV

Think about the shepherd—how he provides for his sheep. How he finds them water without parasites to quench their thirst. How he'll walk miles to

lead them to grass that will nourish them and give them strength.

The gentle shepherd knows when his sheep need rest, and he watches over them while they sleep. With him, they don't fear predators, because he's a strong, skilled protector. Neither do they despair when the terrain is too difficult, because they know the shepherd won't fail them.

Today your Good Shepherd is with you—so don't be afraid. Trust his perfect leadership and unfailing love to keep you, and follow him confidently every day of your life.

God, thank you for being my faithful, compassionate,
and wise Shepherd. I will follow you and trust your
loving provision and protection. AMEN.

Surely goodness and mercy shall follow me all the days of my life, and I shall dwell in the house of the LORD forever.

PSALM 23:6 ESV

IT'S ENOUGH

*The earth is the LORD's, and all it contains, the
world, and those who dwell in it.*
PSALM 24:1 NASB

When the Philistine army slew thirty thousand of
Israel's soldiers and carried away the holy Ark of the
Covenant, the Israelites despaired of ever getting it
back. The Philistines were far too powerful—and the
Israelites too discouraged.

Fortunately, God is never
without resources. Through
a miraculous series of
events, God convinced the
Philistines to bring the Ark
back to Israel.

Tradition holds that
David wrote Psalm 24 to honor the Ark's return to
Jerusalem. Israel learned firsthand that God had all
the resources necessary to help them.

Today embrace that message. Whatever your need,
God's provision is more than enough to help you.
He's in control; trust him to turn everything around
for you.

*God, thank you for reminding me that you're in
control—there's no need or foe I should fear.
Thank you for providing for me. AMEN.*

GOD is at their side; with GOD's help they make it.

PSALM 24:5 MSG

KNOWING HIS SECRETS

*The secret counsel of the LORD is for those who
fear Him, and He reveals His covenant to them.*
PSALM 25:14 HCSB

A strange and wonderful thing occurs as you
spend time with God—circumstances begin to make
sense to you that never did before. Your spirit

 becomes sensitive to the important details of life, and you can
discern how certain situations will
turn out.

This is not about supernatural
premonitions. Rather, your heightened perception has to do with
understanding God's will for
you—seeing his activity in your life
with spiritual eyes.

When your gaze is fixed on the Lord, you know
where he's taking you, what he's teaching you, and
the ways he's transforming your life. So spend time
with him every day and allow his wisdom to shed
light on your path.

*God, I look forward to spending time with you and
learning your ways. I love you and want to know you
with all my heart. AMEN.*

Show me your ways, O LORD, teach me
your paths; guide me in your truth and
teach me, for you are God my Savior,
and my hope is in you all day long.

PSALM 25:4–5 NIV

Never Be Shaken

The LORD's plans stand firm forever; his intentions can never be shaken.

PSALM 33:11 NLT

NECESSARY ANALYSIS

*Examine me, GOD . . . Make sure I'm fit inside
and out so I never lose sight of your love,
but keep in step with you.*
PSALM 26:2–3 MSG

Sometimes you'll be surprised at the temptations
you succumb to. In fact, you may be shocked at what

you're capable of—especially if
you're doing your best to honor
God. How can you fight those
enticements?

The first step, of course, is to
confess what you've done and
receive God's forgiveness. Yet
there's a second thing you
should do—allow God to
search you and reveal what makes those temptations
appealing to you.

When you invite God's analysis, he can reveal the
needs deep within you—those you may not even
realize you have—that are causing trouble. Then he
can fill those needs in a constructive way, and ultimately save you a lot of heartache.

*God, I do want to honor you. Examine me—reveal
the deep needs within me so that I can
love you with my life. AMEN.*

*I will walk in my integrity;
redeem me and be merciful
to me. My foot stands in an
even place; in the congrega-
tions I will bless the LORD.*

PSALM 26:11–12 NKJV

DON'T CHARGE AHEAD

*Wait for the LORD; be strong, and let your heart
take courage; wait for the LORD!*
PSALM 27:14 ESV

At times the doors of opportunity don't seem to open
fast enough—especially when your need is great. You
come to the edge of your wits, strength, and resources;
you wonder if there's something else you could do to
improve your situation.

The great temptation is
to disregard God's leadership and forge ahead, creating your own mediocre
solutions. However, the
doors of God's best blessings can't be forced open.

There are times for stepping out in faith and times
for patience—and God will show you what is necessary for your situation. Even so, listen to God, take
heart, and trust him. No one can close the doors of
blessing God has for you.

*God, I will be patient and listen to you—I won't
charge ahead. Your timing is perfect and I thank
you that the blessings you have for me
are mine forever. AMEN.*

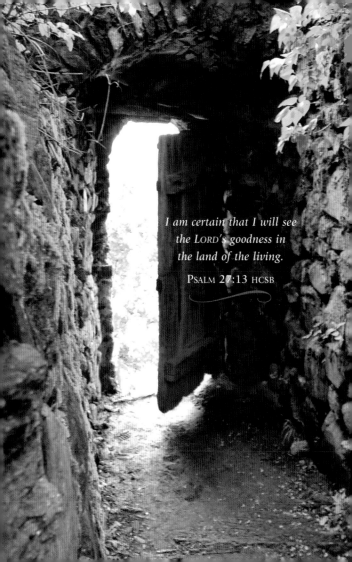

*I am certain that I will see
the LORD's goodness in
the land of the living.*

PSALM **27**:13 HCSB

JUST TRUST—REALLY

*The LORD is my strength and my shield; in him
my heart trusts, and I am helped; my heart
exults, and with my song I give thanks to him.*
PSALM 28:7 ESV

The psalms are all about trusting in God. That's
because they were written by real people who had

real emotions about real struggles.
When they cried out to the living
God, he truly helped them and vin-
dicated their faith in him.

You shouldn't forget that.
Though the psalms are beautiful
and poetic, they are the authentic
feelings and experiences of people
just like you. Just as the psalmists trusted in God and
saw his victorious provision, so can you.

Whatever you are facing today—anger, apathy,
fear, joy, contentment, or sorrow—there's most likely a psalm that echoes your emotions. And undoubtedly its conclusion is this: trust God. The psalmists
did, and you should too. Really.

*God, thank you for the psalms—the testimonies of
people who trusted you and saw your deliverance.
Truly you are fully trustworthy. AMEN.*

*The Lord is their [unyielding]
Strength, and He is the Stronghold of
salvation to [me] His anointed. Save
Your people . . . nourish and shepherd
them and carry them forever.*

PSALM 28:8–9 AMP

VOICE-QUAKE

*The voice of the L*ORD *is powerful; the voice of*
*the L*ORD *is full of majesty . . . The voice of the*
L*ORD shakes the wilderness.*
PSALM 29:4, 8 NKJV

At the sound of his voice, the winds and the waves
obey and calm down. At his command, the rains fall
or the rivers recede.

He spoke, and day and
night; heaven and earth;
animals, birds, and fish;
flowers, plants, and trees;
and man and woman were
created. He opened his
mouth and the stars
appeared—and the entire universe with them.

When God speaks, all of creation responds and
trembles. His word is powerful—it's the foundation
for everything that exists. So listen to him and don't
be afraid when his voice shakes you. Embrace his
message, because he's creating things for you that are
better than you can imagine.

God, I know your voice is powerful and wondrous! I
praise you for your wonderful word—let me hear you
clearly today, my God. AMEN.

Above the floodwaters is GOD's *throne
from which his power flows, from
which he rules the world.* GOD *makes
his people strong.* GOD *gives
his people peace.*

PSALM 29:10–11 MSG

FROM DESPAIR TO DELIGHT

Weeping may endure for a night,
but joy comes in the morning.
PSALM 30:5 AMP

Everything appears more frightening in the dark. The house that's so warm and inviting while sunlight streams through its windows is ominous during a stormy night. As unknown creaks and groans

echo through the walls, your place of shelter can feel confining and treacherous.

The same is true when there's darkness in your circumstances. The unknown can be fearsome and restrictive, and you long for the light of understanding to shine on your situation.

Don't be discouraged—it's never as bad as it seems. The fresh sunrise will reveal God's insight and provision for your problems. As he illuminates your situation, you'll see that what brought you despair was really an opportunity for delight.

God, I'm counting on you to turn this time of sorrow
into a vehicle of joy. Thank you for shedding light
on my circumstances. AMEN.

*You changed my sorrow into dancing. You took
away my clothes of sadness, and clothed me in
happiness. I will sing to you and not be silent.
LORD, my God, I will praise you forever.*

PSALM 30:11–12 NCV

HE UNDERSTANDS YOUR HURT

*I will be glad and rejoice in your love, for you
saw my affliction and knew the
anguish of my soul.*
PSALM 31:7 NIV

Do you find it difficult to explain everything you're feeling about your circumstances, your disappointments, and the dreams that have taken far too  long to materialize? Truly, who could put words to all the emotions that rise up within you?

Yet there is One who understands every bit of your anguish. Jesus came to earth to experience what you're feeling and to understand your inner struggles. Because of his perfect wisdom concerning you, Jesus knows exactly how to restore your heart and comfort your soul.

So don't be afraid that no one understands what you're going through. Jesus does. Today turn to him and allow him to heal your wounded heart with his love.

*God, thank you for understanding me and healing me
with your love. I'm so thankful that you comprehend
the things there are no words for. AMEN.*

I will praise you, LORD, for showing great kindness when I was like a city under attack. I was terrified . . . But you answered my prayer when I shouted for help.

PSALM 31:21–22 CEV

A COMPLETE FORGIVENESS

Happy is the person whose sins are forgiven,
whose wrongs are pardoned.
PSALM 32:1 NCV

Nobody has to tell you what the worst things you've done are. They burn in your heart, destroying your joy—always condemning you and tainting the  good things you do. Just when you really feel loved by God, an awful thought destroys your peace. *How can God accept me when I've been so wayward?*

Friend, when God forgives you, he does so completely—he makes you absolutely clean. You never have to remember those sins again. He certainly doesn't.

So confess your sins once and for all, and whenever thoughts of your past plague you, think about God's perfect forgiveness. Rejoice that when he looks at you, he sees a person he truly loves.

God, I praise you for not holding my past against me.
I rejoice that you forgive me! Thank you for loving
me and making me new. AMEN.

*I acknowledged my sin to You, and my
iniquity I did not hide; I said, "I will
confess my transgressions to the LORD";
and You forgave the guilt of my sin.*

PSALM 32:5 NASB

UNBREAKABLE

The LORD's plans stand firm forever;
his intentions can never be shaken.
PSALM 33:11 NLT

God has spoken concerning an issue that's very important to you, and he's given you a promise that resonates deep within your soul. You know it's from him because his Word confirms it and his deep 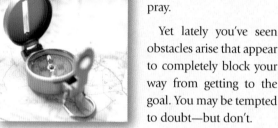 peace fills you when you pray.

Yet lately you've seen obstacles arise that appear to completely block your way from getting to the goal. You may be tempted to doubt—but don't.

No impediment can hinder God's wonderful plans for you. Just like God faithfully fulfilled his covenant to bring the Israelites into the Promised Land, he will carry out his pledge to you as well.

Count on it—God's word to you will never be broken.

God, thank you that your promises to me are completely unbreakable and that the obstacles
before me are nothing to you. I praise
your powerful name! AMEN.

Sing new songs of praise to him; play skillfully on the harp and sing with joy. For the word of the LORD holds true, and everything he does is worthy of our trust.

PSALM 33:3–4 NLT

YOU'RE GLOWING!

They looked to Him and were radiant; their
faces shall never blush for shame or be confused.
PSALM 34:5 AMP

When Moses returned from meeting with God on
Mount Sinai, his face shone so brightly that it aston-
ished the Israelites. Such was the result of being in

God's presence—God's brilliance lingered on Moses'
countenance.

Though your time with
God may be somewhat dif-
ferent than Moses', the lasting effect will nevertheless
be the same: God's glory
will show through you. You
may not notice any difference when looking in the
mirror, but others will see the glow of his likeness in
your spirit and character.

Every time you meet with God, it'll affect you in a
positive way. So spend time with him often and let
the beauty of his radiance shine through you.

God, you bring such light to my life! Thank you for
shining through me. I pray others will see your
glory and love you. AMEN.

My soul will boast in the Lord; let the afflicted hear and rejoice. Glorify the Lord with me; let us exalt his name together.

PSALM 34:2–3 NIV

WHEN YOU'D LEAST EXPECT HIM

The LORD is close to the brokenhearted, and he
saves those whose spirits have been crushed.
PSALM 34:18 NCV

Like most people, you may not seek God's presence when you're feeling low. Beat down, undermined, or simply exhausted, you may question your

worth and judge yourself completely useless to him.

Thankfully, God knows that this is precisely when you need him the most, and he rushes in to comfort you.

Though it's when you'd least expect anyone to be interested in you, God is near when you're crushed and brokenhearted. And it's when you're most vulnerable and powerless that he can be strong for you and others can see him working through you.

So today let God comfort you. His mercy will heal your heart, and others will see his compassion.

God, thank you for loving and comforting me when I
feel worthless and vulnerable. May others see your
powerful love and seek you in return. AMEN.

The LORD's people may suffer a lot,
but he will always bring
them safely through.

PSALM 34:19 CEV

THEIR OPINIONS WON'T STICK

*Rouse yourself, O Lord, and defend me; rise up,
my God, and plead my cause.*
PSALM 35:23 GNT

It's just not fair. You help someone, but they denigrate you in return. You conscientiously do excellent work for someone and get blamed for problems that

aren't your fault. The godly love you've attempted to express has resulted in your disparagement and discouragement.

Does anyone realize the injustice of it all?

Yes, God does. He sees everything you do and knows you're motivated by your love for him.

Though the people you tried to assist have snubbed you, God won't allow their false claims against you to remain.

Their opinions won't stick—so honor him and forgive them. Others will surely see his love flowing through you and will respect you even more.

*God, it is difficult to forgive my detractors, but I will.
Thank you for defending and loving me.
It's an honor to serve you. AMEN.*

May those who delight in my vindication shout for joy and gladness; may
they always say, "The LORD be exalted,
who delights in the well-being
of his servant."

PSALM 35:27 NIV

THE PRICELESS SHADOW

How precious is Your steadfast love, O God! The children of men take refuge and put their trust under the shadow of Your wings.
PSALM 36:7 AMP

Success is invigorating to experience—especially when your dreams are coming true and you soar to new heights. Even so, you need protection when you're achieving your goals, lest you become conceited about your abilities.

Thankfully, God's sheltering wing is your protection against arrogance. Under his glorious wing, you remember that he's the one who has lifted you to the pinnacle and that you're accountable to him for your actions.

Were you to fall from such an elevation due to your pride, you'd be crushed. But God keeps you humble and safe. With him you know that even if you fall, you'll rise again. Surely he's worthy of adoration for the provision of his protective wing.

God, thank you for giving me success and protecting me as my dreams become reality. Truly, you are worthy of all honor, glory, and praise! AMEN.

*Your lovingkindness, O L{ORD}, extends to the
heavens, Your faithfulness reaches to the skies.
Your righteousness is like the mountains . . .
O L{ORD}, You preserve man.*

P{SALM} 36:5–6 {NASB}

DELIGHTING AND REQUITING

Delight yourself in the LORD, and he will give you the desires of your heart.
PSALM 37:4 ESV

There is a desire that germinates in your heart—like a rare, sacred flower it grows and fills you with joy and purpose. The Lord has planted it in you. You made him your focus and delight, and he's given you this special yearning in your soul.

Yet perhaps you're wondering when this sweet promise will bloom—when you will see its wondrous petals of blessing unfold. The days come and go, yet you have no sign of it blossoming.

Friend, the God who sows this hope in you will reap a glad harvest in due time. Just keep enjoying him. Soon enough, the desires of your heart will flourish and you'll rejoice in him anew.

God, you truly are my delight. Thank you for the continued assurance that you will keep your promises to me. I praise your precious name. AMEN.

*Wait for the L*ORD*, and keep His way,*
and He will exalt you.

PSALM 37:34 NASB

ALREADY DONE

*Commit your way to the LORD, trust also in
Him, and He will do it.*
PSALM 37:5 NASB

God anointed David to be ruler of Israel years
before David ever occupied the throne. To David, the
time provided numerous opportunities for ques-

tions and doubts. Often,
David wondered if he'd live
to be king and just had to
trust that God would fulfill
his promise.

Yet to God, this was purely
a training period—there was no question he'd keep
his pledge. God was simply preparing David to
honor him in all the affairs of state.

The point is, what you perceive as a long time of
doubtful unknowns has a purpose to God. His
promise to you is already accomplished. So make
the most of this waiting time by knowing him better.

*God, thank you for putting the times of waiting into
perspective. I praise you that all you've planned
for me is already accomplished. AMEN.*

Be still and rest in the Lord;
wait for Him and patiently
lean yourself upon Him.

PSALM 37:7 AMP

Light of Your Face

*Not by their own sword did they win the land
. . . but your right hand and your arm,
and the light of your face, for you
delighted in them.*

PSALM 44:3 ESV

HE SEES THROUGH THE ACT

*Lord, all my desire is before You; and my
sighing is not hidden from You.*
PSALM 38:9 AMP

We've all done it. Someone asks, "How are you?"
and our automatic answer is, "Fine." Unfortunately,
that's not always true. It's just easier—and safer.

It's intimidating to be
real with people. They may
get offended. They could
criticize you or make you
feel guilty. They could even
use your confessions against
you.

The thing is, you can't
hide your emotions and troubles from God. He sees
the un-sugarcoated truth of your heart and still
accepts you, which means you don't have to fear
communicating openly with him.

You may put on an act with others, but you
shouldn't with God. He knows—and will always
love—the real you. Be honest with him.

*God, thank you for being compassionate and loving
me completely—even the parts that I'm ashamed of.
Help me to be truthful with you in all things. AMEN.*

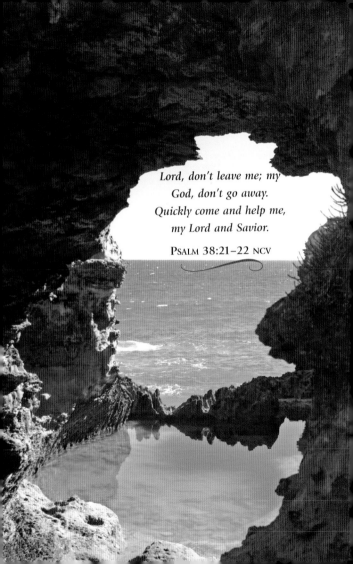

*Lord, don't leave me; my
God, don't go away.
Quickly come and help me,
my Lord and Savior.*

PSALM 38:21–22 NCV

TODAY IS THE GOOD DAY

LORD, remind me how brief my time on earth
will be. Remind me that my days are numbered,
and that my life is fleeing away.
PSALM 39:4 NLT

The calm sea produces a sudden tsunami. The clear, brilliant skies fill with the smoke of an unexpected explosion. The body that appears fit is imperceptibly racked with disease.

These unanticipated calamities shock your soul, but they also infuse you with valuable wisdom: You must appreciate your loved ones today, for you may not have tomorrow.

Friend, no matter what your hopes are for the future, don't wait to start living until you achieve them. Make the most of every moment and care for those around you.

Today is the good day, so honor God by living it out fully. Worship God, love your family, and make it the best day of your life.

God, I thank you for every moment of my life. Help
me to not worry about tomorrow but focus on
honoring you today. AMEN.

"An entire lifetime is just a
moment to you; human existence
is but a breath." . . . And so,
Lord, where do I put my hope?
My only hope is in you.

PSALM 39:5, 7 NLT

WHAT A MESS!

*He lifted me out of the . . . mire; he set my feet
on a rock and gave me a firm place to stand.*
PSALM 40:2 NIV

You've probably heard that old cowboy proverb:
"If you find yourself in a hole, stop digging." It
reflects the principle that if you've created problems
for yourself through your mode of operation, you

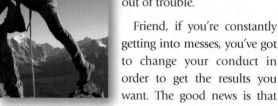

must alter your methods to get
out of trouble.

Friend, if you're constantly
getting into messes, you've got
to change your conduct in
order to get the results you
want. The good news is that
God wants to teach you a new way to do things
that'll satisfy your soul.

Today submit to God's instructions, and he'll
show you his path out of your predicament. He'll
transform the way you think and give you a firm
place to stand.

*God, thank you for getting me out of my hole and
onto your rock! Thank you for transforming my mind
and the way I operate. AMEN.*

He put a new song in my mouth, a
song of praise to our God. Many people
will see this and worship him. Then
they will trust the LORD.

PSALM 40:3 NCV

BETTER THAN YOU CAN IMAGINE

You, Lord God, have done many wonderful things, and you have planned marvelous things for us. No one is like you! I would never be able to tell all you have done.
PSALM 40:5 CEV

What would you like to be doing in ten or twenty years? Perhaps you have a picture in mind of what

the perfect future looks like. Interestingly, many people who achieve all their goals find that their success was not as satisfying as they thought it would be.

Yet there are also those who've forgotten their own plans in order to pursue God. As David testified in Psalm 40, they discover a life full of purpose and love—abundant in hope and wonder.

Friend, you can imagine great things, but God's plans for you are infinitely better than all of them. So pursue and obey him. He'll grant your heart's deepest desires and never disappoint you.

God, I thank you that your plans for me are far better than anything I can envision. I'm excited about the great things you will do. AMEN.

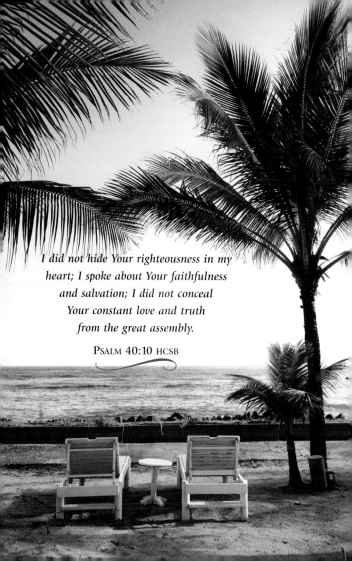

I did not hide Your righteousness in my
heart; I spoke about Your faithfulness
and salvation; I did not conceal
Your constant love and truth
from the great assembly.

PSALM 40:10 HCSB

A PROMISE FOR THE MERCIFUL

How blessed is he who considers the helpless; the
Lord will deliver him in a day of trouble.
PSALM 41:1 NASB

You resemble God's character when you show love
and mercy to someone who is in need. God takes
note each time you allow him to shine through

you—every instance when you
have compassion on others who
cannot help themselves or who
have mistreated you because of
their own inner pain.

Though it's easier to pass them
by—though it's often inconven-
ient and uncomfortable to relate
to people you don't associate with or agree with—
still, that's when you are doing his work in the most
poignant way.

Today remember that you harvest what you plant.
So make it your goal to show mercy wherever you
go, being sure that you'll find it when you're in need.

God, thank you for this wonderful promise. Please
reveal opportunities for me to express mercy today,
and help me to show others your love
and compassion. AMEN.

You will help me, because I do what is right; you will keep me in your presence forever. Praise the LORD, the God of Israel! Praise him now and forever! Amen!

PSALM 41:12–13 GNT

I CAN GET TRUE SATISFACTION

As a deer longs for a stream of cool water,
so I long for you, O God.
PSALM 42:1 GNT

A deer's need for water is never completely gone. Though it may drink and be satisfied for a while, soon enough its body will demand more.

You have similar requirements—though not just

for physical sustenance such as food and water. You need love, acceptance, and purpose. Most of all, your soul must have God.

It's true that you can attempt to fill those needs with other things—relationships, wealth, activities, etc.—but they'll never truly fulfill you. They only mask your true yearning and make you hungrier.

Deep inside, you long for God—and you can have as much of him as your heart can handle. So don't go thirsty. Drink him in and satisfy your soul.

God, I've been filling my soul with other things, but I realize that I really only yearn for you. Please satisfy my hunger with your presence. AMEN.

*My soul thirsts for God, for the living
God. When can I go and
meet with God?*

PSALM 42:2 NIV

DAY AND NIGHT

*The LORD will send His faithful love by day; His song will be with me in the night—
a prayer to the God of my life.*
PSALM 42:8 HCSB

You can't predict when you'll need to be comforted—and neither can your loved ones. You want to talk, but they're unavailable. Perhaps it's because  they're not home or it's just too late to call. Maybe they're facing deep struggles of their own. Whatever the case, they can't help you. Where can you turn?

Day or night, you can always talk to God. Although your confidants may get tired or lack the ability to console you, God never will.

No matter your situation, you can always pray. In fact, God invites you to communicate with him at all times. He wants to be a constant, loving presence in your life—so call upon him frequently.

God, you know the troubles in my soul. Speak peace to me, my God, and help me always turn to you in my time of need. AMEN.

Why am I so sad? Why am I so troubled? I will put my hope in God, and once again I will praise him, my savior and my God.

PSALM 42:11 GNT

HIS WAY IS THE HIGHWAY

Send out your light and your truth; let them guide me. Let them lead me to your holy mountain, to the place where you live.
PSALM 43:3 NLT

It's not about coming up with ways to serve God—what pleases him is that you obey him. He doesn't want a relationship with you based on regulations—

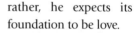

rather, he expects its foundation to be love.

Though it's easier to follow a set of spiritual rules, that's not what God has called you to.

That's why sometimes when you're doing everything "right," God sets you on a darkened path—he's showing you how to rely upon him completely.

God would rather have a healthy, authentic relationship with you than watch you observe some sacred ritual. His way is higher than mere religion, so follow him. He'll teach you to really love him.

God, I praise you for valuing relationships over regulations and love over rituals. Teach me to love you more every day, my wonderful Lord. AMEN.

*I will go to the altar of God, to God
my exceeding joy; and upon the lyre I
shall praise You, O God, my God.*

PSALM 43:4 NASB

BRAGGING RIGHTS

Not by their own sword did they win the land . . .
but your right hand and your arm, and the light
of your face, for you delighted in them.
PSALM 44:3 ESV

It's a trap to believe that the past was "the best of times." You boastfully reminisce about achieving a

certain goal, having a special relationship, or experiencing some smashing victory—and lament that your golden era is gone forever.

Such a view is usually centered on personal triumphs that were always destined to fade. Instead, your focus should be on God, who doesn't grow weaker in you.

Rather, God will work more powerfully through you as you walk with him daily.

Friend, stop bragging about "the good ol' days" and look forward to your magnificent future with God. Your best days are ahead, so praise the One who gives you everlasting life.

God, please help me to let go of the past. Sometimes
it's hard to be optimistic about the future, but I know
I can trust you. AMEN.

*Not in my bow do I trust, nor can my
sword save me. But you have saved us . . .
In God we have boasted continually,
and we will give thanks to your
name forever.*

PSALM 44:6–8 ESV

HOW HE SEES YOU

The king is enthralled by your beauty; honor him, for he is your lord.
PSALM 45:11 NIV

God is not looking at a magazine cover—he's gazing at you and he likes what he sees. He perceives a heart longing to know and obey him, a mind seeking his truth, and lips offering sincere praises. He  observes a soul cleansed by his forgiveness, hands that do his will, and a soul that increasingly bears his image.

Every day he sees you, his beloved, filled with potential—needing his grace, yearning for his presence, and learning his ways. And he is completely enthralled with you.

Friend, God loves you deeply and finds you absolutely beautiful. So gaze back into his adoring face, and realize that your splendor is really a reflection of his.

Oh, Lord God, how wonderful to be seen by you this way! Fill my eyes with your magnificent face and my heart with your wonderful love. AMEN.

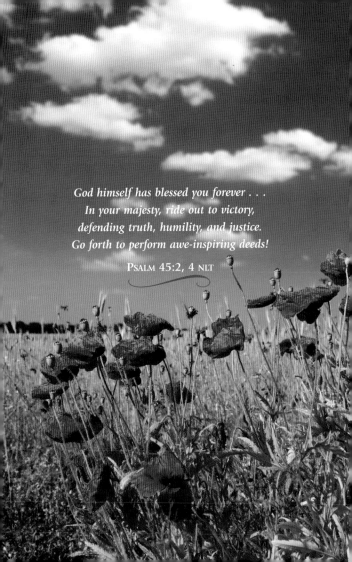

God himself has blessed you forever . . .
In your majesty, ride out to victory,
defending truth, humility, and justice.
Go forth to perform awe-inspiring deeds!

PSALM 45:2, 4 NLT

THOUGH THE WORLD FALLS APART

God is . . . always ready to help in times of trouble. So we will not fear, even if earthquakes come and the mountains crumble into the sea.
PSALM 46:1–2 NLT

As human beings, we tend to describe our security in terms of the earthly things that make us feel safe. Our family, friends, home, job, church, community, and national resources usually comprise our core infrastructure of protection.

But what happens when those things tremble—or worse, tumble? What can we depend on when everything is suddenly taken from us?

You've read enough of this devotional to know that the answer is God—but is that truth ingrained deeply within your heart?

This world was not meant to last. The earth shakes, houses collapse, and businesses fail—they're all temporary. Only God remains trustworthy and steadfast forever. He's the only sure foundation for your security.

God, please help me to base all my confidence in your love and unshakable security. Thank you for sustaining and protecting me. AMEN.

Though its waters roar and foam and the mountains quake with their surging . . . God is within her, she will not fall; God will help her at break of day.

PSALM 46:3, 5 NIV

SEEKING HIM THROUGH THE QUIETNESS

Be still, and know that I am God.
PSALM 46:10 NKJV

We fill our world with noise. If it's not the television or radio, it's the blare of activities or our own anxious thoughts. We expect to connect with God through the tumult, but are we really listening to him?

When your world is in an uproar, your best plan is to step away from the commotion and listen to him. He speaks words of peace to your soul and strength to your life.

Your life is too hectic to keep going without taking a few minutes to seek him in the quietness. Stand in his presence and know that God is with you. His voice is the best sound you'll hear all day.

God, being still doesn't come naturally to me. Please help me to get quiet and really hear you. Thank you for speaking to me. AMEN.

The Lord of hosts is with us; the God of Jacob is our Refuge (our High Tower and Stronghold). Selah [pause, and calmly think of that]!

PSALM 46:11 AMP

GLORY TO THE KING

*God is King of all the earth, so sing a
song of praise to him.*
PSALM 47:7 NCV

Today just think about God—how he is creative
and powerful, wise, holy, and completely faithful.

Consider God's works—how he's helped his
people throughout history. Through his power, the Red

Sea parted for the Israelites, the
walls of Jericho crumbled,
David slew Goliath, and Jesus
was raised from the dead.

Meditate on his character—
how all he does is because of
his unconditional love for you. He is mighty and
good, virtuous and trustworthy, wise and compassionate.

Today think about God and voice your praise to
him out loud. He is the magnificent king of glory
who has plans for you that are better than you can
imagine. Certainly he deserves your adoration.

*Sweetest, most wonderful Lord God, truly you merit my
worship. How good you are and how deep your love—
may the whole world rejoice at your name! AMEN.*

*God ascends amid shouts of joy, the
L*ORD*, amid the sound of trumpets.
Sing praise to God, sing praise; sing
praise to our King, sing praise!*

PSALM 47:5–6 HCSB

FOREVER GOD

This is God, our God forever and ever.
He will guide us forever.
PSALM 48:14 ESV

God exists. Before there was time, God was there. He's as infinitely past as he is eternally future.

If that's a difficult concept for you to grasp, you're in good company. We as human beings are

linear thinkers—we understand things in terms of beginnings and endings. How is it that God was never born? What does it mean that he'll never die?

Yet God is more than all of that. He's above how we function—beyond the constraints of hours, days, and years.

That's why God's wisdom regarding your life can be trusted. He knows everything concerning your past and all about your future. His perspective will never fail you. Listen to him.

God, my mind cannot comprehend you, but my heart
trusts you. Thank you for your perfect perspective. I'm
glad my future is in your hands. AMEN.

We heard about it, then we saw it with our eyes—in GOD's city of Angel Armies, in the city our God set on firm foundations, firm forever. We pondered your love-in-action, God.

PSALM 48:8–9 MSG

Seeking God's Love

*God looked down from heaven on all people
to see if anyone was wise, if anyone was
looking to God for help.*

PSALM 53:2 NCV

RICHES OF KNOWING

*My mouth shall speak wisdom; and the
meditation of my heart shall be understanding.*
PSALM 49:3 AMP

Investments come in all shapes and sizes, but they
generally share one goal: to produce wealth.
Unfortunately, they also have one end in common:
they don't last forever.

Thankfully, there is a type
of asset that doesn't rust or
fade—that others cannot steal
or manipulate. Instead, it is
eternal because it's an invest-
ment in the kingdom of God.

Every moment you spend
in God's presence—praying to him, worshiping him,
knowing him, studying his Word, and obeying him—
you're becoming rich in treasure that's everlasting.

True wisdom and wealth are found in seeking God
and understanding his ways. So invest yourself in
knowing and serving God. A life based on him will
never be misspent.

*God, I want to be a wise investor. Grant me the
riches of knowing you more deeply during
my times in your presence. AMEN.*

Man, despite his riches, does not
endure . . . . But God will redeem
my life from the grave; he will
surely take me to himself.

PSALM 49:12, 15 NIV

GIFTS OF GRATEFULNESS

*He who sacrifices thank offerings honors me,
and he prepares the way so that I may
show him the salvation of God.*
PSALM 50:23 NIV

God doesn't need your thanks, praise, or adoration. He doesn't need an ego boost or validation.  Rather, God asks you to express your gratefulness because of what it means to your own soul.

It's in those moments of thanksgiving when you realize that he's the source of all your blessings—and that they're not given because of your worthiness, but because of his love for you. As your words echo back into your ears that God is the great Provider, his power fills you, and your heart is transformed.

So sing out your gratefulness to God. Thank him for his goodness to you. Undoubtedly, the one who'll be most blessed is you.

*God, there's so much to thank you for: my life and
family, provisions and blessings. But most important,
thank you, God, for loving me. AMEN.*

*I am God Most High! The only
sacrifice I want is for you to be
thankful and to keep your word. Pray
to me in time of trouble. I will rescue
you, and you will honor me.*

PSALM 50:14–15 CEV

ADMITTING HE'S RIGHT

Against you, you only, have I sinned and done what is evil in your sight, so that you may be justified in your words and blameless in your judgment.
PSALM 51:4 ESV

One of the most difficult aspects of having a relationship with God is realizing that he knows what's

best for you. That's why he will point out destructive habits or mistakes in your life and invite you to agree with him that you have a problem. He doesn't want you to feel ashamed about it; rather, he wants you to get better.

Friend, you need to admit to God that you're struggling with your situation before he will start the process of healing you. Then God will unearth the causes of your troubles and restore you—he'll make you feel clean and new. So do it—admit he's right. You'll be glad you embraced the healing that sets you free.

God, this is difficult, but I trust you and admit you're right. I praise you for being compassionate as you reveal my sins and heal me. AMEN.

God, be merciful to me because you are loving. Because you are always ready to be merciful, wipe out all my wrongs. Wash away all my guilt and make me clean again.

PSALM 51:1–2 NCV

WHAT HE ACCEPTS

The sacrifices of God are a broken spirit; a broken and a contrite heart, O God, You will not despise.
PSALM 51:17 NASB

God will never kick you when you're down. He won't look at you when you're feeling tired and unworthy and say, "What's the matter with you? Try harder!"

God isn't looking for impressive feats of showmanship from you; rather, he's looking at the attitude of your heart. He has compassion for you when you've failed, and he treats your wounded spirit with love.

God accepts you, friend, just as you are. Don't ever fear that you're not good enough for him, because that's not what God is interested in. He just wants you to be eager to obey him and willing to trust him more. Because then you're truly a person he can work with.

God, thank you for accepting me and handling my broken heart with kindness. I am eager to obey and willing to trust you. AMEN.

Create in me a clean heart, O God.
Renew a right spirit within me . . .
Restore to me again the joy of
your salvation, and make
me willing to obey you.

PSALM 51:10, 12 NLT

HOW TO THRIVE

I am like a flourishing olive tree in the house of God; I trust in God's faithful love forever and ever.
PSALM 52:8 HCSB

Have you received an assignment that's less than thrilling? Are you discouraged because it seems beneath your expertise and training? Then you're thinking about the wrong thing. Instead of focusing  on the negative aspects of the task, consider these questions: "Why has this duty come to me? Why does it require my attention?"

Perhaps you've received it to model godly character to someone else, or because you must learn some humility. Possibly, the task is more important than you realize, or maybe it's God's provision for your bills.

Whatever the reason, it's an opportunity for excellence. So don't be discouraged. Rather, honor God with your assignment. No doubt, you'll be glad you did.

God, please help my attitude. I don't know your purpose for this task, but I'll do my best to honor you and thrive in it. AMEN.

I will praise You forever for what You have done. In the presence of Your faithful people, I will put my hope in Your name, for it is good.

PSALM 52:9 HCSB

WHO IS WISE?

*God looked down from heaven on all people to see
if anyone was wise, if anyone was
looking to God for help.*
PSALM 53:2 NCV

When reading Psalms, perhaps you've noticed that
Psalm 53 is very similar to Psalm 14. Why, then,
would it be included in the Bible? British minister

Charles Spurgeon explains,
"[God's Word] never repeats
itself needlessly, there is good
cause for the second copy of
this Psalm."

The truth is that sometimes—
even though we trust God—we
fail to seek him. We forget the
many times he's helped us. That's why we need this
psalm repeated—to remind us to look to him
continually.

To be truly wise is to seek God in every situation.
Do you have some need today? Seek him. He's
always ready to extend his aid and loves it when
you ask.

*God, thank you for always being ready to help me.
Please increase my wisdom by continually reminding
me to seek you. AMEN.*

God restores the fortunes of his people.

PSALM 53:6 ESV

THEY ARE NOT SO STRONG

You have rescued me from all my troubles, and I have seen my enemies defeated.
PSALM 54:7 GNT

As David and his weary men fled from King Saul's relentless forces, they came to the Desert of Ziph, hoping they could hide and get some rest. Unfortunately, the people there were Saul's allies,  and they divulged David's covert location. Saul's soldiers closed in on David and all seemed lost.

Whenever difficulties close in on you, you may feel as David did—defenseless, drained, and discouraged. Everything will seem to be working toward your defeat.

Yet you must understand that God showed himself stronger than Saul's army—they were forced to abandon their pursuit of David. No matter how tough your problems are, they're never as mighty as God. Trust and obey him—you'll surely see your troubles defeated.

God, I praise you that you're always mightier than my problems. Thank you for helping me and for leading me to victory. AMEN.

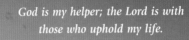

God is my helper; the Lord is with those who uphold my life.

PSALM 54:4 NKJV

HE DOESN'T TIRE

At dusk, dawn, and noon I sigh deep sighs—
he hears, he rescues.
PSALM 55:17 MSG

There are circumstances that will consume every bit of your energy. They're real and pressing, all-consuming and painful. No matter what you do, your situation is in the forefront of your mind. You simply can't shake it.

Your loved ones may be supportive, but you cannot expect them to comfort you every time the anxieties surface or the tears begin to flow. They get weary and so do you.

It's in those times that you must draw upon God's comfort, strength, and wisdom. Others will let you down, but God never will. So call upon his unflagging love morning, noon, and night—whenever you need him. He is always ready to help you.

God, I praise you for being my tireless Comforter,
Provider, and Friend. Thank you, God, for
hearing me whenever I call to you. AMEN.

As for me, I will call upon God, and the LORD shall save me.

PSALM 55:16 NKJV

SHIFTING THE PILE

Pile your troubles on GOD's shoulders—he'll carry your load, he'll help you out. He'll never let good people topple into ruin.
PSALM 55:22 MSG

You should always make your loved ones a priority in your life. Yet you must also understand that sometimes God will use circumstances to prevent you  from helping them when they're struggling.

Whether it's because of distance, health, responsibilities, or even relational barriers, God may have allowed the separation to keep you from interfering in what he's teaching them. You may want to shoulder a burden that only he can carry for them. Or perhaps he is refining their character through their troubles.

Whatever the case, you must shift your worries about them to God. Always remember that he's able to care for them better than you are. Just keep praying and let him work.

God, it's rough seeing loved ones making bad decisions or suffering, but I trust you to work in them. I pray they'll depend on you. AMEN.

*Evening and morning and at noon I will
pray, and cry aloud, and He shall hear my
voice. He has redeemed my soul in peace.*

PSALM 55:17–18 NKJV

WHEN FEAR COMES CHARGING IN

When I get really afraid I come to you in trust.
PSALM 56:3 MSG

Fear is a powerful, unreasonable emotion. It influences how you think and react, and it even affects your physical well-being. Fear will stop you from  reaching your potential or from allowing your loved ones to be all they can be. You know God is directing you in a certain way, but you refuse to step out in faith because of your apprehensions.

Understand that your fear is based on an expectation of punishment—you believe it's inevitable that only bad things will happen. Instead, you must focus on God's character. God is all-powerful, all knowing, and completely loving. So obey him—he'll only lead you in what's best for you. With God, you never have to be afraid.

God, fear is a powerful influence in my life. Help me to obey you in faith and trust you whenever my anxieties come charging in. AMEN.

*In God, whose word I praise, in God I
have put my trust; I shall not be
afraid. What can mere man do to me?*

PSALM 56:4 NASB

YOUR PROTECTED PURPOSE

I cry out to God Most High, to God who fulfills his purpose for me.
PSALM 57:2 ESV

You'll come to places that seem like abrupt ends to your dreams. Every door will appear closed, and you may even have to accept responsibilities that seem completely incompatible with the promises God has

given you. Before you begin to think, *It's all over*, remember that only this portion of your journey has concluded.

Don't despair. God is developing your character and strengthening your faith. The purpose for your life is so important that God himself protects it for you—you don't have to fear that it's been lost or ruined forever.

So no matter how long it takes, obey and follow God without wavering. Despite the detours, he'll unfailingly lead you to your purpose.

God, thank you for protecting my future and for leading me to your purpose for my life. Help me to follow you obediently and without wavering. AMEN.

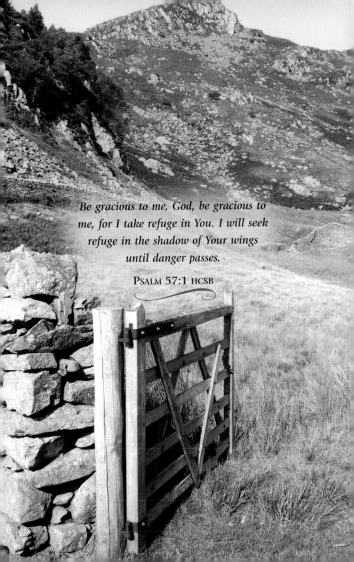

Be gracious to me, God, be gracious to
me, for I take refuge in You. I will seek
refuge in the shadow of Your wings
until danger passes.

PSALM 57:1 HCSB

NOT IN VAIN

Everyone will say, "It's true! Good people are rewarded. God does rule the earth with justice."
PSALM 58:11 CEV

Serving God isn't easy. You'll encounter trouble from the strangest places. You'll try to help people, and others will criticize what you're doing. You'll  work long years trying to make a difference, but you won't see the outcome you expected.

Yes, serving God is difficult—but friend, it's wholeheartedly worth it. You see, there's a great reward for those who do God's work on earth. Not only is God pleased while you're obeying him, but you'll see the fruit of your labor in heaven.

All the love you pour out will generate unimaginably wonderful results in God's kingdom. So have faith and keep serving him. You'll never find a better return for your work.

God, keep me strong as I serve you. Remind me that it's not about seeking others' approval or earthly rewards, but about glorifying you. AMEN.

*The godly will rejoice when they
see injustice avenged.*

PSALM 58:10 NLT

WATCHING

I will keep watch for You, my strength,
because God is my stronghold.
PSALM 59:9 HCSB

When learning to draw, you're taught a new way to see—you observe light, shadow, perspective, and depth in order to make your portraits realistic.

The same concept is true in your spiritual life. You may be very good at assessing your earthly landscape, but if you fail to notice what's happening spiritually, you're only getting half the picture. That's why you must watch for God's activity.

Friend, what you see with your physical eyes is temporary, but what you perceive God doing in your spirit is eternal. So ask God to open your spiritual eyes to his supernatural work. When you learn to observe his ways, you'll undoubtedly view life a lot more clearly.

God, please open my spiritual eyes so that I can see
your wonderful, eternal ways. I'll keep watch for you,
my God, because you are my strength. AMEN.

You've been a safe place for me . . .
Strong God, I'm watching you do it, I
can always count on you—God, my
dependable love.

PSALM 59:16–17 MSG

HIS BANNER OVER YOU

You planted a flag to rally your people, an unfurled flag to look to for courage.
PSALM 60:4 MSG

Though he'd successfully conquered many of the surrounding territories, King David was not prepared for this military tactic. As he fought the Arameans in the north, the Edomites executed a surprise attack from the south.

Of course, David was humble about his triumphs—always attributing them to God's banner of protection. So God rewarded him with victories over both armies.

You'll certainly face times of success when unexpected problems sneak up from behind and stun you. That's why David instructs you to always look to God's banner for your courage. When God is your strength and focus, you cannot fail.

Victory comes from God—so keep your eyes on him. He'll certainly honor you for it.

God, I look up to your banner—my focus on your unfailing character. You are always my protection and hope. Thank you for leading me to triumph! AMEN.

With God we will gain the victory.

PSALM 60:12 NIV

Robed With Strength

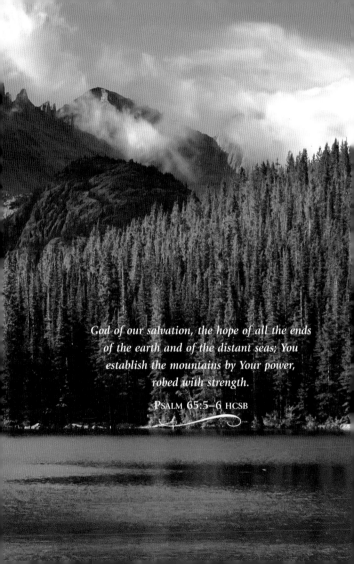

*God of our salvation, the hope of all the ends
of the earth and of the distant seas; You
establish the mountains by Your power,
robed with strength.*

PSALM 65:5–6 HCSB

A HERITAGE OF FAITH

*You, O God, have heard my vows; You have given
me the heritage of those who fear Your name.*
PSALM 61:5 NKJV

Hopefully you're trusting in God for your struggles
today. One wonderful way to strengthen your confidence in him is to consider the people who've served
God before you.

Whether your parents and
grandparents knew God or
not, you have a heritage of
faith to encourage you.
Throughout the Bible are his-
tories that'll fill you with awe
at the power and faithfulness
of God. Yet you'll also observe what others have trusted
God for—things beyond human imagination—and
how they were rewarded.

You're not alone in your relationship with God. From
Genesis to Revelation you will find outstanding exam-
ples of overcoming faith and answered prayer. Ours is a
heritage to be proud of—so read on and be inspired.

*God, thank you that the Bible was written for my
encouragement and is a record of your faithfulness
throughout history. You are worthy of great praise! AMEN.*

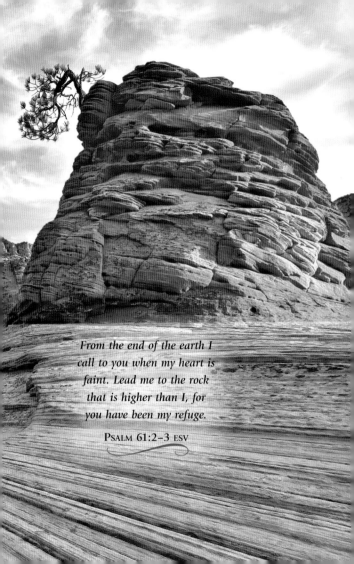

From the end of the earth I call to you when my heart is faint. Lead me to the rock that is higher than I, for you have been my refuge.

PSALM 61:2–3 ESV

RESTORATIVE HOPE

I find rest in God; only he gives me hope.
PSALM 62:5 NCV

Have you gotten to the point that you feel you can't continue? Sometimes this is because of legitimately strenuous tasks. But more often than not, this happens when you handle your responsibilities in your own strength.

You keep working and pushing—feeling that if you fail, everything will fall apart. You trust yourself for success rather than God—and it's wearing you out.

Friend, you need to rest and trust that God will reenergize and inspire you. He'll show you how to work smarter—instead of harder—and accomplish everything in his strength.

So take a break and let him restore you. He'll fill you with his wisdom and empower you for all your tasks.

God, it's hard to let go because there's so much to do.
Help me to trust you, and please multiply
my times of rest. AMEN.

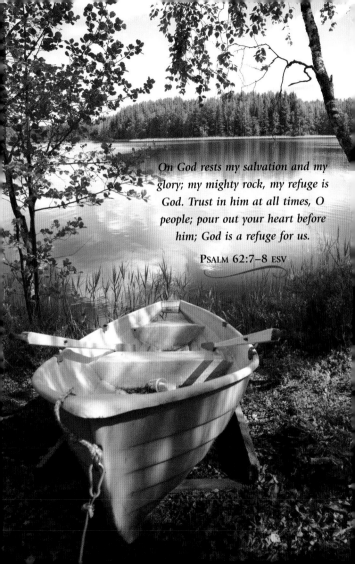

On God rests my salvation and my glory; my mighty rock, my refuge is God. Trust in him at all times, O people; pour out your heart before him; God is a refuge for us.

PSALM 62:7–8 ESV

A BANQUET FOR YOUR SPIRIT

*My soul will feast and be satisfied, and I will
sing glad songs of praise to you.*
PSALM 63:5 GNT

Is there a need inside you that just can't be satisfied? It can't be filled by food, possessions, or entertainment—you've tried it all and it's all failed.

It may be that the part that's calling out to be fed is your soul. There is within each person an appetite for God that can only be satisfied in his presence. Whether in prayer, worship, Bible study, or service, your soul must be nourished by God.

Perhaps you don't really believe this, so here's a challenge for you: The next time you feel that longing, allow your soul to be filled by God. Undoubtedly, you'll find that he was what your spirit was seeking all along.

*God, you say that those who hunger for righteousness
will be satisfied and blessed. Fill my emptiness, God.
Only you can fill my heart with joy. AMEN.*

I am in the place of worship, eyes
open, drinking in your strength
and glory. In your generous love I
am really living at last! My lips
brim praises like fountains.

PSALM 63:2–3 MSG

SLEEPLESS

I remember you while I'm lying in bed;
I think about you through the night.
PSALM 63:6 NCV

The clock is ticking louder than usual. The bed doesn't feel right either. You toss and turn, trying to get comfortable. Eventually you realize that what's  really making you restless are your maddening thoughts.

Your mind is on and you can't stop what's rushing through it— worry after worry bombards you without respite. You try to think of something else, but the anxieties come back even louder than before.

When you're sleepless, friend, turn your thoughts to God and think about all he's done for you. Pray to him and give him all your concerns. Make your wakefulness into a worshipful time with him. He'll surely calm your soul and lead you into true rest.

God, only you can bring tranquility to my barrage of thoughts. Bring rest to my sleepless soul. I know that I'm safe within your loving care. AMEN.

You have been my help, and in the shadow of your wings I will sing for joy. My soul clings to you; your right hand upholds me.

PSALM 63:7–8 ESV

NO CONTEST

Then everyone will stand in awe, proclaiming
the mighty acts of God, realizing
all the amazing things he does.
PSALM 64:9 NLT

It's all about getting ahead. You must prove yourself to be the best—whether it's through your intellect, beauty, wealth, or skills. People are naturally  disposed to comparing themselves to others—to competing and seeking prominence at whatever they consider their strength.

But you don't have to put yourself through such a useless and destructive exercise. God loves you just the way you are. He's given you unique talents that he's going to work through, so you don't have to contend against other people—you can work with them.

Friend, don't compete. When God is working through you, you're already the best you can be. You're already a winner, so be gracious and act like it.

God, I want to feel special. Help me to realize that
it's you who makes me unique, successful, and
loved—and not how I compete. AMEN.

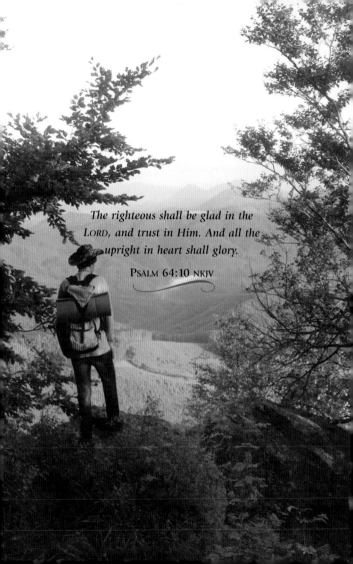

The righteous shall be glad in the LORD, and trust in Him. And all the upright in heart shall glory.

PSALM 64:10 NKJV

CREATOR AND SUSTAINER

*God of our salvation, the hope of all the ends of
the earth and of the distant seas; You establish the
mountains by Your power, robed with strength.*
PSALM 65:5–6 HCSB

Have you ever wondered why God created the
earth—laying its foundation with such ingenuity
and care? Have you considered why he'd fill it with

such a variety of birds, animals,
and fish? Why he'd create mountains and valleys, rivers and seas?
Why there would be such different seasons and climates, colors
and foliage?

Friend, God did it for you.
God filled the world with wonder and sustenance not only to
feed your stomach, but to nourish your imagination
and soul.

So praise your magnificent Creator and Sustainer,
who has constructed this amazing world. Surely, the
One who's done all this is mighty and is able to care
for all of your needs.

*God, you are astounding and majestic—your creation
inspires my soul. Thank you, God, for filling the
world with such imaginative creatures and
beautiful landscapes. AMEN.*

You care for the land and water it; you enrich it abundantly. The streams of God are filled with water to provide the people with grain, for so you have ordained it.

PSALM 65:9 NIV

CHOICES

If I had been cozy with evil,
the Lord would never have listened.
PSALM 66:18 MSG

Whenever you make a choice, you declare what's important to you and progress in a definite direc-

tion. This is because you've either elected to honor God or serve something else.

What about the mundane choices? Does it matter where you eat lunch or what you wear to work? In such cases, it's always best to ask yourself, *Is there anything about my selection that God would object to?*
Are there any godly principles that would help me pick a better alternative?

Often, it's not the major decisions that change the course of your life, but the little ones you make daily. So honor God with all your choices—his way will always be your best option.

God, teach me the principles that will help me make
the best choices, and help me to honor you in all my
decisions—even the mundane ones. AMEN.

*Let the whole world bless our God and loudly
sing his praises. Our lives are in his hands,
and he keeps our feet from stumbling.*

PSALM 66:8–9 NLT

TIME FOR THE HARVEST

Then the earth will yield its harvests,
and God, our God, will richly bless us.
PSALM 67:6 NLT

Any farmer who plants seeds in the ground and then returns the following day expecting to see a full-grown crop is quite foolish. Unfortunately, many of us assume our prayers will produce results in much the

same way. We ask God for the deepest desires of our heart, and then we become frustrated when our prayers aren't answered immediately.

Though we want instantaneous results, God doesn't operate that way. Rather, he gives his best blessings time to mature—to become satisfying to your soul. He also prepares you to receive them.

Friend, God's timing is perfect, so keep praying and be patient. Your harvest of blessing will surely bloom when the time is right.

God, help me to be patient and not lose heart as I
wait for your promises to develop. Thank you for
always giving me your best. AMEN.

*May God be gracious to us and bless
us; look on us with favor . . . so that
Your way may be known on earth,
Your salvation among all nations.*

PSALM 67:1–2 HCSB

ISOLATED NO MORE

A father to the fatherless, a defender of widows,
is God in his holy dwelling. God sets
the lonely in families.
PSALM 68:5–6 NIV

There were none more helpless in ancient society than the widows and orphans. The laws often left those who lost loved ones without much recourse or

hope. So God took care of them—he became their Provider and Defender.

God knows that when you're alone, the world can be a difficult place—but you don't have to continue feeling lonely, isolated, or helpless. God loves you

and invites you to be part of his family. He gives you people to love, who'll love you in return.

So continue to know God and embrace others who belong to his family. As you give of yourself, your loneliness will melt away and your joy will surely grow.

God, thank you for your love and for inviting me to
be part of your family. I praise you for being my
Provider and Defender. AMEN.

The God of Israel is He who gives strength and power to His people. Blessed be God!

Psalm 68:35 NKJV

WEIGHTY CHALLENGES

Blessed be the Lord, who daily bears our burden.
PSALM 68:19 NASB

Loads get heavier the longer you carry them. This is true of both physical weight and emotional responsibilities. The more time you contend with them, the more fatigued you become.

You may believe that you've gotten accustomed to your burdens—that you can handle them—but they're still draining you. You know that because of how difficult it is for you to deal with new challenges. When you stop having joy, it's obvious you're not managing your problems successfully.

Friend, you don't have to be self-sufficient. God is happy to carry your burdens. He'll be your unfailing strength and will use the weight to help you grow. Trust him with your concerns.

God, I'm not quite sure how to give my burdens to you—please show me how. I truly want to trust you with them. AMEN.

Summon your might, O God. Display your power, O God, as you have in the past.

PSALM 68:28 NLT

THE PART THAT COMES ALIVE

*You who seek God, inquiring for and requiring Him
[as your first need], let your hearts revive and live!*
PSALM 69:32 AMP

There are hidden treasure troves within you—
wonderful gold mines of potential that you may not
even know about. God created them within you, and

he's the only one who can
access them. They can only be
cultivated and utilized by
spending time with him.

You undoubtedly have
many talents, but there's even
more within you—aptitudes
that are inspired and empow-
ered solely by God's Spirit. He
makes those hidden abilities

come alive and fills you with meaning and purpose
through them.

So discover the abundant life God created you
for—spend time with him and allow him to make
you into all you can be. You'll discover that there's
more to you than you thought.

*Thank you, God, for giving me such wonderful gifts
and seeing all the potential in me. I praise you for
helping me experience your abundant life. AMEN.*

As for me, I will pray to you, LORD;
answer me, God, at a time you choose.
Answer me because of your great love,
because you keep your promise to save.

PSALM 69:13 GNT

WHAT TO PRAY

May all who seek you rejoice and be glad in you! May those who love your salvation say evermore, "God is great!"
PSALM 70:4 ESV

You may struggle with how to pray for others—especially if they're facing challenging circumstances.

You want God's will to be accomplished, because you know that ultimately it'll be best for them. Yet you don't want them to experience hardship. What do you do?

Pray that whatever God's plan is for them, they'll trust him more through it, and they'll find joy and strength in him and seek him daily. Pray they'll know for certain that he's great, loving, and wise.

Whatever your loved ones are facing, your best prayer for them is that they'd know him better. May all who seek him rejoice and say evermore that God is truly good.

God, I do pray that my loved ones would know you better and trust you more today—no matter what their circumstances. Truly, you are wonderful! AMEN.

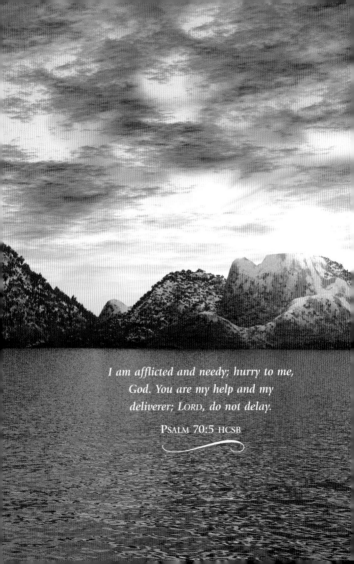

I am afflicted and needy; hurry to me,
God. You are my help and my
deliverer; LORD, *do not delay.*

PSALM 70:5 HCSB

WHY, GOD?

You have allowed me to suffer much hardship,
but you will restore me to life again and
lift me up from the depths of the earth.
PSALM 71:20 NLT

We ask it as a rhetorical question because we don't really expect God to answer. "Why, God?" we call out—voicing more frustration and confusion over our hurt than real inquiry.

Yet realize that God has permitted your hardship for a reason—it isn't random and God isn't being unkind. Though God doesn't *cause* all of your troubles, he *allows* them so you'll trust him more and discover his abundant life.

God uses everything that comes into your life for good. So when you cry out to him for wisdom, expect him to answer. And even if he doesn't give you understanding immediately, be confident that he's got an important reason for all he allows.

God, thank you for using everything for good in my
life—even what I'm facing now. It gives
me hope for the days to come. AMEN.

God, your justice reaches to the skies.
You have done great things; God, there
is no one like you . . . You will make
me greater than ever, and you
will comfort me again.

PSALM 71:19, 21 NCV

GREAT PEOPLE, GREAT RESPONSIBILITIES

Give the gift of wise rule to the king, O God,
the gift of just rule to the crown prince.
PSALM 72:1 MSG

Friend, if you want to be truly great, you must start now by being honorable with all of your obligations. Practice the standards that God instructs in his

 Word—even for the smallest tasks—and he'll give you wisdom and success in the challenges ahead.

Because the more you rise in reputation and power, the more complicated your responsibilities and decisions will be. But if you're guided by godly principles, the right course of action will be clear.

You'll be entrusted with more as you show that you've been faithful with the duties you've been given. So honor God right where you are. People will see you're reliable and will reward you with their trust.

God, teach me to obey your principles so that I can do
my work wisely and honorably. May my life
glorify you in everything I do. AMEN.

*Let him be honest and fair with all
your people, especially the poor. Let
peace and justice rule every mountain
and hill. Let the king defend the poor,
rescue the homeless.*

PSALM 72:2–4 CEV

Wonderful Things

We will tell the next generation about the
LORD's power and his great deeds and the
wonderful things he has done.

PSALM 78:4 GNT

GIVING OUT

My flesh and my heart may fail, but God is the strength of my heart and my portion forever.
PSALM 73:26 ESV

No matter how you add it up, there's no way your resources will stretch any more. You've done all you can, and you're exhausted.

 Like a traveler in the desert with an empty canteen, you're out of options. You can't go on in these conditions, and any hope of finding an oasis of relief has dissipated like a mirage.

The only thing left is to throw yourself onto the mercy of God.

Good—now he can work. As long as you can accomplish something in your own strength, you'll always doubt whether your deliverance was from God or if you achieved it yourself. Your resources have failed, but his haven't. Trust him to help you.

God, I praise you for your mercy. I don't know how you'll help me, but I'm thankful that you will. I'm so glad you're in control. Amen.

It is good for me to draw near to God; I have put my trust in the Lord God and made Him my refuge, that I may tell of all Your works.

PSALM 73:28 AMP

THE ESTABLISHMENT OF BOUNDARIES

You set all the limits on the earth.
PSALM 74:17 NCV

Fire is a wonderful thing—especially when cooking food or keeping warm. Unfortunately, if a fire gets out of control in your home or a forest, it can be devastating. The flames quickly consume everything in their unhindered path.

To avoid disaster, one must only build fires within the confines of a suitable fireplace or pit, where they can be easily managed.

Likewise, boundaries keep the resources and relationships of your life from becoming damaging. That's why God gives you his commands; he knows that too much of a good thing can be harmful, and he wants you to flourish rather than self-destruct.

So don't be afraid of his laws—they'll always keep you safe.

God, thank you that your boundaries are not meant to limit me but protect me. Help me to always abide by your life-giving commands. AMEN.

*You have been our king from the beginning,
O God; you have saved us many times.*

PSALM 74:12 GNT

TIMING IS EVERYTHING

*You say, "I choose the appointed time;
it is I who judge uprightly."*
PSALM 75:2 NIV

Have you ever been the right person in the right place at the right time? When it happens it's quite unexpected. All your circumstances align in a way

 that's unimaginable, and you realize that something greater than yourself must be controlling every element of your situation. Your experiences have all prepared you for this in a way that you couldn't have anticipated.

That's how God works, friend. He works in a way that when everything's done, there's no other explanation for the outcome other than his perfect timing. So don't worry about the things you have to wait for—just obey God with confidence. Because when the right moment comes, you'll certainly be ready.

God, I don't know why I've waited so long, but I praise you that when the right moment comes, I'll know it was your perfect provision. AMEN.

*We thank you, God, we thank you—
your Name is our favorite word; your
mighty works are all we talk about.*

PSALM 75:1 MSG

WHOM TO PLEASE?

You, are to be feared [with awe and reverence]!
PSALM 76:7 AMP

Generally, people are either leaders or followers. Those who serve like to give of themselves, but are often pulled in a hundred directions—trying to please everyone. Those who lead can be inspirational to others—but they sometimes become too self-important.

For both these groups, it's exceedingly important to remember whom they're trying to please—the only One truly worthy of their honor and praise.

For leaders, they must remember that God is the ultimate authority. Those who follow must serve out of obedience, rather than a desire to be accepted.

Friend, whether you're a leader or a follower, God is the only One you'll ever need to please. So honor him with all you do.

God, I want to be a delight to you. Please forgive me for the times when I lose focus. Help me to honor you and bless others. AMEN.

*Make vows to the Lord your God and
fulfill them; let all who
are around Him bring gifts to
Him who is to be feared.*

PSALM 76:11 NASB

THINK ABOUT IT

I will think about all that you have done;
I will meditate on all your mighty acts.
PSALM 77:12 GNT

You wouldn't willingly drink water that had toxins in it; you'd find clean water to relieve your thirst. You probably wouldn't eat food that was poisoned either.  Rather, you'd wrestle with your hunger until you found wholesome sustenance.

Is the same true of your mind?

Perhaps you supply your brain with negative, chewed-over thoughts of hurt. Or maybe boredom—a sign your intellect is starved—causes you to dine on whatever junk comes along. Unfortunately, these diets aren't beneficial at all.

Friend, be careful what you feed your mind—consume only what's good, healthy, and holy. Nourish your understanding with God's Word. It's the only cuisine that'll truly satisfy your mental hunger.

God, please cleanse me of the rubbish in my thoughts.
Help me to feed on your Word so I'll be healthy
in my body, mind, and soul. AMEN.

I will remember your great deeds, Lord; I will recall the wonders you did in the past.

PSALM 77:11 GNT

YOUR LEGACY

*We will tell the next generation about the
LORD's power and his great deeds and the
wonderful things he has done.*
PSALM 78:4 GNT

People often ponder what they'll accomplish in
the future. Yet sometimes it's good to ask: When I
pass away, what story will be told? Will I be remem-

 bered for wisdom and mercy—or
manipulation and self-centered-
ness? Will I leave a lasting legacy
—or will my endeavors fade like
the morning fog?

As you contemplate stepping
into eternity, you'll think about
what's truly important. No one
ever plans to waste his or her life, but it'll happen if
you fail to set priorities.

So consider: What will you leave behind for those
you love? Will your life testify to the eternal love of
God—or the temporary things of this world? Your
story is still being told, so choose wisely.

*Lord God, I want to leave a lasting legacy of love for
you. Please direct my steps so that you'll always
be glorified in my life. AMEN.*

He instructed our ancestors to teach his laws to their children . . . In this way they also will put their trust in God and not forget what he has done, but always obey his commandments.

PSALM 78:5, 7 GNT

AN ISSUE OF TIME

*He remembered that they were only human, like
a wind that blows and does not come back.*
PSALM 78:39 NCV

Have you ever faced a puzzle that seemed completely unsolvable—but then something shifted
your perspective and altered your understanding of

it? Suddenly, you saw the
answer clearly. It was there all
along, but you couldn't grasp it
until your vantage point
changed.

Often, we cannot understand
God's direction because of our
perspective on time. We deal
with issues in the present and
are quick to categorize things as
"deal with now" or "wait until later." Unfortunately,
that's not always the right viewpoint.

What God is doing in you isn't about "now versus
later," but "temporary versus eternal." So don't fight
him—he's teaching you to see life as you've never
understood it before.

*God, thank you for showing me that my human view-
point is limited. Help me to see all of my circumstances
from your outlook—the eternal perspective.* AMEN.

They repented and sought God earnestly.
They remembered that God was their
rock, the Most High God their redeemer.

PSALM 78:34–35 ESV

AN EYE ON THE GUIDE

He led them on safely and in confident trust,
so that they feared not; but the sea
overwhelmed their enemies.
PSALM 78:53 AMP

When God brought the Israelites out of Egypt, he led them with a pillar of cloud by day and a tower of fire by night. These shielded the Israelites from their

enemies and reminded the people of God's powerful presence with them.

Looking to God is an important principle that can keep you from becoming disheartened. As long as you maintain your focus on God, you'll be safe and con-fident. Yet take your eyes off of God, and you'll be overwhelmed by the troubles surrounding you.

Friend, whatever you are facing today, take no heed of the impossibilities. Keep your gaze fixed solely on God. He'll lead you safely through if you'll just believe in him.

God, thank you for helping me with my troubles
today. They overwhelm me, but I am comforted
by your strength and loving presence. AMEN.

*[God] led His own people forth like sheep
and guided them [with a shepherd's care]
like a flock in the wilderness.*

PSALM 78:52 AMP

LINGERING LIABILITIES

Do not punish us for the sins of our ancestors.
Have mercy on us now; we have lost all hope.
PSALM 79:8 GNT

Even the best families can have destructive cycles. These are habits, beliefs, and ways of thinking that hinder you from becoming all that God created you

to be. In a sense, they are liabilities that are passed down through the generations because they are never taken to the One who can heal them.

Yet you can break the destructive cycle because God will teach you a different way to live—he'll have mercy on you and give you the strength and hope you need.

So don't be impeded by the mistakes or deficiencies of your ancestors, and don't let those liabilities linger any longer. Let God make you part of his family—healthy, holy, and free.

God, you know the failings of my family and how those failings have affected me. Heal me and teach me to live in a manner worthy of your name. AMEN.

*Help us, O God of our salva-
tion, for the glory of Your
name; and deliver us, and
provide atonement for our sins,
for Your name's sake!*

PSALM 79:9 NKJV

LIGHT IN THE DARK PLACES

*O God of hosts, restore us and cause Your face
to shine upon us, and we will be saved.*
PSALM 80:7 NASB

What is it that you don't want anyone to know
about? It'll immediately spring to mind because
shame is powerful that way. It convinces you to hide
in self-defeating ways.

Friend, whatever you con-
ceal with darkness will control you. You'll guard it fiercely
because it's painful and
embarrassing; and when anyone gets close to discovering
your defect, you'll get com-
bative. Your anger is based on
the fear that you'll be exposed—and it's destroying
you.

It's scary to invite God's light into your deepest
secrets—but it's the only way that you'll be free. So
don't let the darkness imprison you. Confess your failings to God, and allow him to lead you into the light.

*Oh, God, forgive my sins and bring light to my
darkest secrets. Heal me, my God, and set me
free. Thank you for helping me. AMEN.*

We shall not turn back from you; give us life, and we will call upon your name! Restore us, O LORD God of hosts! Let your face shine, that we may be saved!

PSALM 80:18–19 ESV

OPEN UP!

*I am the LORD your God, who brought you out
of the land of Egypt; open your mouth
wide, and I will fill it.*
PSALM 81:10 NKJV

Psalm 81 was written in celebration of Israel's miraculous deliverance from Egypt. It's a reminder that God's powerful provision is always available for

his people—but we must obey him.

You may be tempted to disregard God and handle your serious situation on your own. Just remember that whenever the people of Israel did that, they got into progressively worse trouble. It was only when they trusted God that they entered the Promised Land.

What needs do you have today? Friend, don't handle them on your own. God will help you and provide for you if you'll be humble enough to admit you need him.

Therefore, open up to God—he's got exactly what you need.

God, I'm so used to handling things on my own. Yet I'm open to your provision and love. Please teach me how to obey you. AMEN.

"I lifted the burden from your shoulder
and took the heavy basket from your
hands. When you were in trouble, I
rescued you, and from the thunder-
clouds, I answered your prayers."

PSALM 81:6–7 CEV

Sing for Joy

*Satisfy us in the morning with Your
lovingkindness, that we may sing
for joy and be glad all our days.*

PSALM 90:14 NASB

THE UNFORGOTTEN

*Defend the weak and the orphans; defend
the rights of the poor and suffering.*
PSALM 82:3 NCV

If I were gone, would anyone notice? Even if you've
never thought those words, you can understand the
sentiment behind them. Sometimes people feel so

powerless and insignifi-
cant that they wonder if
anyone cares for them at
all.

God does not forget
them, and neither should
you. In fact, God may be calling you to be his repre-
sentative of love and support to them.

Who do you know that needs a friend? Rather
than forget about them, find out what you can do to
better their situation. Sometimes your listening ear,
willing heart, and prayers can encourage a person
more than you realize. Because of you, they'll know
that God hasn't forgotten them.

*God, is there someone you want me to help today?
Please bring them to my mind and show me
how to love them as you would. AMEN.*

*Rescue the weak and
needy; deliver them out of
the hand of the wicked.*

PSALM 82:4 NASB

TALK TO ME!

O God, do not keep silent;
do not be still, do not be quiet!
PSALM 83:1 GNT

Why is it that at times God appears to be altogether quiet? Even though you are seeking him wholeheartedly, why does it seem like he's gone completely silent?

Friend, you desire to hear God, and that's wonderful. However, there are times when his silence will do more to grow your faith than anything else. That's because you must continue to do as he instructed and exercise your trust without any outside encouragement.

It's difficult, but you can depend on his trustworthy character and lean on his truth, love, and grace. Take heart—he's still working on your behalf. And when you see how much he's done for you, it'll speak volumes to your soul.

God, even if I can't hear you, I trust you. Thank you
for your faultless character and for continuing
to work on my behalf. AMEN.

May they know that You alone—whose name is Yahweh—are the Most High over all the earth.

PSALM 83:18 HCSB

HIS LOVELY DWELLING PLACE

*A day in your courts is better
than a thousand elsewhere.*
PSALM 84:10 ESV

You've thought about God entering into your situation, now imagine dwelling in his. Picture his glorious home in heaven where there's no suffering or sadness—no tears, troubles, or regrets. It's far more lovely, wondrous, and opulent than anything could ever be here on earth.

Contemplate living in God's joy and peace for all eternity—together with loved ones you'll never be separated from again. Visualize praising him with people from every nation who are also filled with adoration for him.

God is preparing you for his everlasting kingdom and constructing a special place for you that you can forever call home. So begin knowing and worshiping him now—you can't ever have too much practice!

You are the living God and I praise you! I yearn to live in your presence and worship at your footstool, my glorious God. AMEN.

How lovely is your dwelling place, O LORD Almighty! My soul yearns, even faints, for the courts of the LORD; my heart and my flesh cry out for the living God.

PSALM 84:1–2 NIV

WORDS OF PEACE

I will hear what God the Lord will say; for He will speak peace to His people, to His godly ones.
PSALM 85:8 NASB

Worrying is a difficult habit to break—especially because it's become such an inherent part of you. "Worrying—a habit? Impossible! It's part of my nature!" you may exclaim.

No, friend. Worrying reflects how your mind has been conditioned—not the way you've been created. Remember that when you worry, you're declaring that God is not going to help you. You doubt him, his character, and his love.

However, God wants you to trust him, and his message to you is peace. He doesn't want you to worry but to be confident in his care. So listen to his words and learn from him. He'll help you break that bad, worrisome habit and live with confidence.

God, please forgive me for doubting. I want to trust you. Please transform the way I think so I won't fret but will always hope in you. AMEN.

The Lord will indeed give what is good, and our land will yield its harvest. Righteousness goes before him and prepares the way for his steps.

Psalm 85:12–13 NIV

YOU ARE RIGHT TO ASK

*Protect me and save me because you are my
God. I am your faithful servant, and I trust you.*
PSALM 86:2 CEV

Why must you pray? If God already knows all your
needs and heart's desires, why is it necessary to ask
him to fill them?

Friend, God wants you to ask
for his help because it opens the
lines of communication. He
wants to have a relationship
with you. If he were to satisfy
your needs without you ever
asking, you'd never remember
to interact with him. Yet when you pray to him, you
open yourself to his love and provision.

So pray—and do it often. Get to know the Lord
God and let him into your life. He'll not only be
your Provider, he'll be your Counselor, Confidant,
King, and Friend.

*God, thank you for wanting a relationship with me.
I want to know you too. Help me to seek you
and love you more every day. AMEN.*

Be kind to me! I pray to you all day. Make my heart glad! I serve you, and my prayer is sincere. You willingly forgive, and your love is always there for those who pray to you.

PSALM 86:3–5 CEV

UNDIVIDED, UNENCUMBERED

Teach me Your way, LORD, and I will live
by Your truth. Give me an undivided
mind to fear Your name.
PSALM 86:11 HCSB

You've heard it said that you cannot serve two masters. And it's true. When your heart is divided

between two goals—or two leading influences—you will not have peace. They'll always battle against each other to hold you, which will encumber you with inner conflict.

Friend, do you have something in your life that is competing with God for your affections? Ask yourself: What does it offer that God cannot provide? What need does it fill that God cannot satisfy better?

You'll undoubtedly find that whatever your second master is, it falls short of God's promises to you. So leave it behind. You'll only be truly free when your devotion is completely undivided.

God, give me an undivided heart to love and obey
you. May nothing ever come between us, but
help me to honor you with my life. AMEN.

There is no god like you and no works like yours. Lord, all the nations you have made will come and worship you. They will honor you . . . Only you are God.

PSALM 86:8–10 NCV

DO YOU REALIZE IT?

Wonderful things are said about you.
PSALM 87:3 NCV

It's interesting that people who genuinely follow God often don't know what a blessing they are to others. They've been taught to be humble—to hold God as their standard instead of others—so they're modest about their graces and abilities.

Friend, if you've been seeking God obediently, he's been shining through you. His unique qualities of love, joy, peace, patience, kindness, gentleness, and faithfulness have encouraged others and inspired them to seek God.

The humility you experience isn't about feeling worthless; it's about attributing the glory in you to God. So if you're feeling down about yourself—stop it. You just can't see what others can. God is working through you, and that's truly praiseworthy.

Wow, God. Thank you that the good others see in me is you! Thank you for shining through me and giving me your beautiful attributes. AMEN.

Of Zion it shall be said . . . The Most
High himself will establish her.

PSALM 87:5 ESV

STARTING THE DAY WITH HIM

*To You I cry, O Lord; and in the morning
shall my prayer come to meet You.*
PSALM 88:13 AMP

If you were a soldier, you wouldn't leave home without suiting up for war. You'd be sure you had your orders and all the equipment you needed to successfully engage the battles ahead.

Though you may not be a conventional warrior, you've got conflicts to face throughout the day—struggles you're not quite sure how to handle. You'll also have unforeseen skirmishes with others, and you'll wrestle with strategic situations that will require ingenuity, strength, and wisdom.

That's why you should always start your day with God and commit all its troubles to his hands. Remember that all your battles belong to him. As your Commander, he'll always lead you safely to triumph.

God, I'm glad you know what today holds. Thank you for equipping me with everything I need to face everything that's ahead. You're truly wonderful! AMEN.

Lord, you are the God who saves me. I
cry out to you day and night. Receive
my prayer, and listen to my cry.

PSALM 88:1–2 NCV

YOUR LIFE IS A PSALM

Happy are those who hear the joyful call to worship, for they will walk in the light of your presence, LORD.
PSALM 89:15 NLT

When you believe in God, your life is a psalm—one that will be read throughout eternity. It will record your downbeats of doubt as you cry out to  God with your troubles. And it will chronicle your chords of exultation as he helps you and gives you the desires of your heart.

The theme of your life will be God's faithfulness to you, for when all your days have been documented, you will undoubtedly report that he never failed you.

Your life is a song of praise to God that's being written through your circumstances. Today find peace in the knowledge that he's making your life into a beautifully intricate work of art.

God, thank you that every exultant high note and dissonant chord in my life is making a beautiful song of praise to your faithfulness. AMEN.

*Because of you they rejoice all day
long, and they praise you for your
goodness. You give us great victories;
in your love you make us triumphant.*

PSALM 89:16–17 GNT

GOD'S DIFFERENT PERSPECTIVE

*To you, a thousand years is like the passing of a
day, or like a few hours in the night.*
PSALM 90:4 NCV

God has not failed you. Though every human
indicator may suggest that God is absent from your
situation, the reality is far from it. The problem is

that the full panorama has
yet to be seen—your com-
plete situation still hasn't
been unveiled.

Why has God allowed
these trials to come into
your life? It's not because
he is letting you down.
Rather, he's teaching you
that he makes all your circumstances work together
for your good—even the waiting.

So don't fret. Hang on to him as tightly as you can
and trust that he's working out something important. Because when you see what he sees, you're
going to love the big picture.

*God, I know you won't ever let me down. Help me
hang on until I can see your answer to my
prayers. I know you're faithful. AMEN.*

Give us gladness in proportion to our former misery! Replace the evil years with good. Let us, your servants, see you work again; let our children see your glory.

PSALM 90:15–16 NLT

BETTER THAN BREAKFAST

*Satisfy us in the morning with Your
lovingkindness, that we may sing
for joy and be glad all our days.*
PSALM 90:14 NASB

A healthy breakfast has many benefits—it'll help
you have better strength, endurance, concentration,
productivity, and creativity. Yet there's nothing as

positive or energizing as feed-
ing on God's Word in the
morning.

God knows what you need
before you ever get out of
bed; when you spend time
with him, he nourishes you
with the perfect diet of joy, wisdom, and strength to
fuel you throughout the day.

So before you pour the cornflakes or gulp down
that cup of java, remember that your spirit needs to
be fed too. Enjoy a hearty helping of God's presence
early each morning. You really will be starting your
day in the very best way.

*God, thank you for nourishing my spirit with the
perfect diet for today's activities. May I honor you
with my strength, endurance, concentration,
productivity, and creativity. AMEN.*

*Lord our God, may your blessings be
with us. Give us success in all we do!*

PSALM 90:17 GNT

EVERLASTING CONFIDENCE

Those who live in the shelter of the Most High
will find rest in the shadow of the Almighty.
PSALM 91:1 NLT

Danger. It's a word that raises your anxiety level because of its dire implications. Dangers threaten your life and those of your loved ones. Dangers shake your

world and destroy your security. Dangers make you question everything—especially why God would allow them.

Yet when you know God and trust him for salvation, perils can only come so near to you because God protects your eternal destination. Though hazards may trouble you on earth, you can be confident that they won't follow you into heaven.

So don't fear the dangers. Rather, thank God that the worst that can happen is limited—and it's nothing compared to the wonderful things he's planned for you.

God, I face many dangers every day, but none are
stronger than you. Thank you for protecting me and
my loved ones daily and for eternity. AMEN.

You have made the LORD, my refuge, even the Most High, your dwelling place. No evil will befall you, nor will any plague come near your tent.

PSALM 91:9–10 NASB

PRAISE ALL DAY?

*LORD Most High! It is wonderful each morning
to tell about your love and at night to
announce how faithful you are.*
PSALM 92:1–2 CEV

When speaking with others, do you assume the
best—or the worst? Are you pessimistic in your dis-
course or positive? Friend, your conversation is self-
fulfilling.

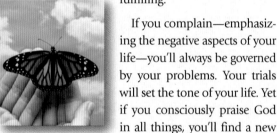

If you complain—emphasiz-
ing the negative aspects of your
life—you'll always be governed
by your problems. Your trials
will set the tone of your life. Yet
if you consciously praise God
in all things, you'll find a new
confidence and strength that nothing can take away.
With him, truly nothing will be impossible for you.

This isn't a naïve optimism. Rather, it's the deep-
seated understanding of God's unfaltering love and
faithfulness. So yes, friend, praise him all day,
because every day you experience God's presence is a
good one.

*God, I do praise you! Thank you for working through
my positive attitude to bring glory to yourself—
and strength and joy to me. AMEN.*

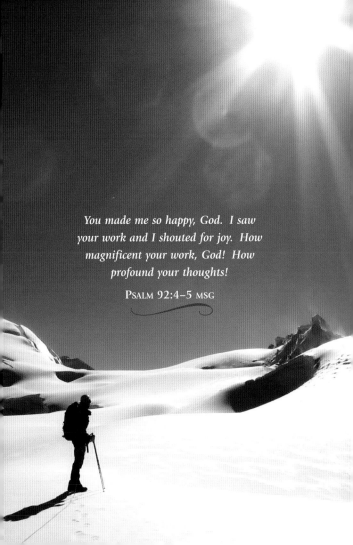

You made me so happy, God. I saw your work and I shouted for joy. How magnificent your work, God! How profound your thoughts!

PSALM 92:4–5 MSG

UNCHANGING

God is King, robed and ruling, God is robed and surging with strength. And yes, the world is firm, immovable, Your throne ever firm—you're Eternal!
PSALM 93:1 MSG

It seems that everything changes—and, in a sense, everything in this world is fleeting. Earthly things just weren't intended to last forever.

Like a flower, we see living things germinate, grow, bloom, and then begin the process of decay. Even our lives are ruled by time—births and deaths, beginnings and endings. The cycles of change are inherent in our nature.

Yet God isn't subject to any such phases or cycles. Immune from time, God's character is completely unchanging and his nature is eternal. That's why as things start, finish, and change in your life, you can always hope in him. God will always be steadfastly faithful to you—today, tomorrow, and always.

Oh, how I need you, God! Thank you for being unchanging, immovable, and wise. Thank you for always providing stability and strength to my life.
AMEN.

What you say goes—it always has.
"Beauty" and "Holy" mark your palace
rule, God, to the very end of time.

PSALM 93:5 MSG

SPIRITUAL WORKOUT

How blessed the man you train, God, the
woman you instruct in your Word.
PSALM 94:12 MSG

Spiritual lessons require practice—that's the simple truth of the matter. You may believe you know everything necessary about faith or obedience; yet

almost as soon as you express your confidence about that area, you're plunged headlong into a situation that puts your understanding to the test.

Don't be surprised—it's through this process that what you've learned intellectually becomes a practical reality in you. It's like a physical workout—your knowledge of the machines at the gym means nothing until you put it to use and actually do the exercises.

So today thank God for training you through your trials and strengthening your spiritual muscles. It's preparation that you'll certainly be glad to have.

God, thank you for stretching my faith in you and
making it real. Thank you for always loving me and
comforting me in every circumstance. AMEN.

*The minute I said, "I'm slipping, I'm falling,"
your love, God, took hold and held me fast.
When I was upset and beside myself, you
calmed me down and cheered me up.*

PSALM 94:18–19 MSG

BE WILLING

Today, if you hear his voice,
do not harden your hearts.
PSALM 95:7–8 ESV

No way! It may be the first thing you think when you understand God's will for you. Maybe that's because his plans seem overwhelmingly difficult, or

because they involve too many of your weaknesses. Perhaps it's because God's directions seem counter to your own ideas or prejudices. Whatever the reason, you really don't want to do as God says.

Reconsider, friend—don't be so quick to say no. God wants to do great things through you—endeavors that will astonish your eyes and bring true joy to your soul. True, it's going to take faith, but if you're willing to do whatever God says, you're sure to be blessed. So say yes, and trust him.

God, I do want to obey you, but I'm afraid. Fill me
with confidence in your ways so I may serve you
faithfully and please you. AMEN.

The LORD is a great God and a great
King above all gods . . . Come, let us
worship and bow down, let us kneel
before the Lord our Maker.

PSALM 95:3, 6 NASB

WHAT CAN'T HE DO?

Ascribe to the LORD, you families of the peoples,
ascribe to the LORD glory and strength.
PSALM 96:7 HCSB

It might surprise you to find out that there are things God cannot do. Though God is all-powerful, there are certain acts he won't commit because of his character.

For example, God is holy, so he cannot lie or break his promises to you. He'll never use his knowledge for evil—he'll only use his great wisdom to help you.

God cannot stop loving you either, because love is his nature. Yet because of that, he can't stand silently by when you take a destructive path. That's why he offers you his salvation— because he wants you to spend eternity with him.

So embrace God and trust his ways. He can't fail you—isn't that wonderful?

God, I praise you for your holy, loving ways.
Thank you that I can always count on you.
You couldn't be more wonderful!

AMEN.

Sing to the LORD and praise his
name; every day tell how he saves us
. . . He is coming to judge the world;
he will judge the world with fairness
and the peoples with truth.

PSALM 96:2, 13 NCV

Shout Praises

Shout praises to the LORD,
everyone on this earth. Be
joyful and sing as you come
in to worship the Lord!

PSALM 100:1–2 CEV

SCARY WORLD, STRONG GOD

*Love the L*ORD *and hate evil! God protects his
loyal people and rescues them from violence.*
PSALM 97:10 CEV

The pressure is always there—you must play along
to get along. You do things that you aren't comfortable with in order to please others. You know that

what you should do is
stand up for what's
right, but you feel so
helpless. What choice
do you really have?

Friend, understand
that you're never alone.
Though you're afraid of
crossing someone who could hurt you or mess up
your future, realize that God will always honor you
for doing what is right.

God is with you and he's powerful. The people
harassing you may prosper in the short term, but not
forever. So trust God and obey him. He'll surely
show himself mighty on your behalf.

*God, thank you for being with me in this situation.
It's difficult to obey you, but I will. Protect me and
help me do what's right. A*MEN.

If you obey and do right, a light will show you the way and fill you with happiness. You are the LORD's people! So celebrate and praise the only God.

PSALM 97:11–12 CEV

HIS LOVE IS WITH YOU

*He has remembered his love and his loyalty to
the people of Israel. All the ends of the earth
have seen God's power to save.*
PSALM 98:3 NCV

God loves you, and that love is unlimited. You
may have to earn love from others—or even work
hard to maintain it. But not for God's love. He offers

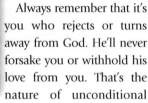

it to you freely and never
stops caring for you.

Always remember that it's
you who rejects or turns
away from God. He'll never
forsake you or withhold his
love from you. That's the
nature of unconditional
love—it's given because it flows from God's character and has absolutely nothing to do with your
actions. His love is always with you, in hopes that
you'll receive it.

So embrace God's love. Forget your fears and feel
its overwhelmingly wonderful power. Then, love
him back.

*My God, I do love you! Thank you for loving me
unconditionally and for giving me the victory and
salvation because of your powerful love. AMEN.*

Sing a new song to the LORD, for he has done
wonderful deeds. His right hand has won a mighty
victory; his holy arm has shown his saving power!

PSALM 98:1 NLT

WORSHIPING HOLINESS

*Exalt the LORD our God, and worship at his holy
mountain; for the LORD our God is holy!*
PSALM 99:9 ESV

God is holy—he embodies holiness. Several
words may come to your mind such as sacred,
blessed, and virtuous. Yet you may also wonder what
exactly all that means.

God's holiness means
that he's free from
problems common to
mankind and earthly lim-
itations. He has no imper-
fections. Also, God is
diametrically opposed to
evil—he always does what is good and loving and never
has moral dilemmas. Though he allows bad things to
happen for now, he won't permit them for-ever. God
faithfully fulfills all his promises.

God is set apart—higher, purer, and more wonderful than all you know. And yet he still loves and helps
you. Surely, that makes him worthy of your worship.

*Yes, Lord, you are worthy of my worship and awe. I
praise you for being sacred, blessed, virtuous, pure,
perfect, and good. Truly, you are holy!* AMEN.

The Lord is great in Zion, and He is high above all the peoples. Let them confess and praise Your great name, awesome and reverence inspiring! It is holy, and holy is He!

PSALM 99:2–3 AMP

A GLOBAL SONG

*Shout praises to the LORD, everyone on this
earth. Be joyful and sing as you come
in to worship the LORD!*
PSALM 100:1–2 CEV

Who could imagine one thing that everyone on
earth could agree upon? With all of the cultures,
languages, and traditions—how could we come to
 an understanding about
anything?

Yet we are told that one
day every knee will bow
and every tongue will confess Jesus as Lord. One day
we will join hearts and
hands with brothers and
sisters across the world with one purpose: to praise
the One who saves us. What economics, politics, and
diplomacy could never achieve will happen naturally
because of the extraordinary love of Jesus.

So anticipate the global chorus by praising him
today. And thank him that one day it'll be a song the
whole world will sing.

*Jesus, I praise you that the day is coming that people
from every nation will sing your praise! You
are truly worthy, my Savior! AMEN.*

Acknowledge that the LORD is God. He made us, and we are His—His people, the sheep of His pasture. Enter His gates with thanksgiving and His courts with praise.

PSALM 100:3–4 HCSB

THE GOOD LIFE

*I will give heed to the blameless way. When will
You come to me? I will walk within my house
in the integrity of my heart.*
PSALM 101:2 NASB

King David knew what it was like to be a poor shepherd boy and a wealthy king. He'd experienced what it was to have nothing and to have everything—to be lowly and unnoticed and to have the respect and love of a nation.

Yet through it all, there was one thing that defined the worthwhile life to David—a healthy relationship with God.

No matter how you define "the good life," one thing is certain: It's always better with God. As David discovered, possessions and power will fail to satisfy your soul, but God never will.

God can fill you with more joy and purpose than anything you can imagine. So follow him to the best life.

*God, you make my life so much better. Lead me to
the life you have for me—I know it's more wonderful
than I can imagine! AMEN.*

I will sing of your love and justice; to you, O Lord, I will sing praise.

Psalm 101:1 NIV

THE TIME FOR FAVOR

I pray to you, LORD! Please listen. Don't hide from me in my time of trouble. Pay attention to my prayer and quickly give an answer.
PSALM 102:1–2 CEV

If you've ever seen a baby bird wrestling free from its egg or a butterfly escaping its cocoon, you know it's a long, arduous process. Yet it's completely neces-

sary because the creatures must become strong enough to endure conditions outside of their protective coverings.

Friend, have you likewise suffered a lengthy, difficult delay in seeing God's promises fulfilled? Understand that God doesn't make you wait in vain—it's necessary for you to be prepared for your blessings. The longer you wait, the more precious and beautiful God's provision will be.

So count this time as one of training and favor— because you can be sure that God is doing wonderful and important things in your life.

God, help me to trust you and persevere during this time. It's really been a struggle, but I know that your blessings are worth the wait. AMEN.

You will arise and have compassion on Zion, for it is time to show favor to her; the appointed time has come.

PSALM 102:13 NIV

ARE YOU MAD?

*The Lord is merciful and gracious, slow to anger
and plenteous in mercy and loving-kindness.*
PSALM 103:8 AMP

Do you know people who are angered by the littlest things? It seems like they're always offended about something, and you're never sure how to please them.

Sometimes that kind of personality is attributed to  God because of his multitude of instructions in the Bible. Yet nothing could be further from the truth. God gives you rules because he loves you— not because he's easily offended. He knows a holy life will ultimately be happier and healthier for you.

God doesn't get angry as quickly or easily as people do. Rather, he always treats you with compassion and grace. So don't fear that you've made him mad. Instead, rejoice that he loves you deeply.

*God, thank you for your love, compassion, and grace.
Thank you for being patient with me and for always
forgiving me when I confess my offenses. AMEN.*

The LORD is like a father to his children,
tender and compassionate to those who
fear him. For he knows how weak we are.

PSALM 103:13–14 NLT

FAR ENOUGH

How far has the LORD taken our sins from us?
Farther than the distance from east to west!
PSALM 103:12 CEV

You fail and it plagues you. You make a mistake and cringe at what God must think. Other people don't let you forget your wrongdoing—so why should God?

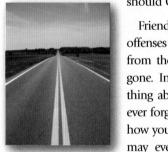

Friend, once you confess your offenses to God and turn away from them, they're completely gone. In fact, they're the only thing about you that God will ever forget. You may remember how you've disobeyed him and may even have to face some consequences, but God forgives you completely and refuses to recall the iniquities you've committed.

East and west will never meet, and you'll never have to face your sins again. So forgive yourself and thank God that when he removes your transgressions, they're erased forever.

God, thank you for forgetting my wrongs and treating me with mercy and grace. Thank you for your uncon- ditional love and unfailing forgiveness. AMEN.

Praise the Lord, my soul, and do not forget how kind he is.
He forgives all my sins and heals all my diseases. He keeps
me from the grave and blesses me with love and mercy.

PSALM 103:2–4 GNT

UNLIMITED, BREATHTAKING WISDOM

What a wildly wonderful world, God! You made it all, with Wisdom at your side, made earth overflow with your wonderful creations.
PSALM 104:24 MSG

Currently, there are an estimated nine thousand species of birds known in the world. What is more,

there are over fifteen thousand kinds of mammals, in excess of twenty-nine thousand types of fish, and more than thirty million varieties of insects.

Though these numbers are bound to increase as new discoveries are made, God knows them all and provides for their needs. Nothing is born, grows, or dies without God knowing it.

Yet there's a magnificent creature that gets God's special attention—you. He's as careful with the minutiae in your life as he was in creating the microscopic attributes that make one species different from another.

His wisdom helps you perfectly. Awesome, isn't it?

God, I'm in absolute awe of your great wisdom, understanding, and creativity. Thank you for being so profoundly involved in every area of my life. AMEN.

These all wait for You, that You
may give them their food in
due season . . . You open Your
hand, they are filled with good
. . . May the glory of the LORD
endure forever.

PSALM 104:27–28, 31 NKJV

RULE NUMBER ONE

Seek the LORD and his strength;
seek his presence continually!
PSALM 105:4 ESV

As David wrote this psalm about Israel's journey to the Promised Land, he knew one very important thing to be true: Whenever people would turn to God and obey him, he would help them achieve vic-

tory. This was a principle that David was committed to because he'd seen God lead him to so many triumphs.

That's why rule number one for you is this: Seek God and do as he says. Not only will God guide you in your circumstances, but you'll know him even better.

So as situations arise today—negative or positive— look to God and obey him. It's a simple rule, but it's one that will assuredly bring you joy and success.

God, help me to love you so much that I automatically
seek and obey you in every circumstance. Thank you
for showing me the way to victory. AMEN.

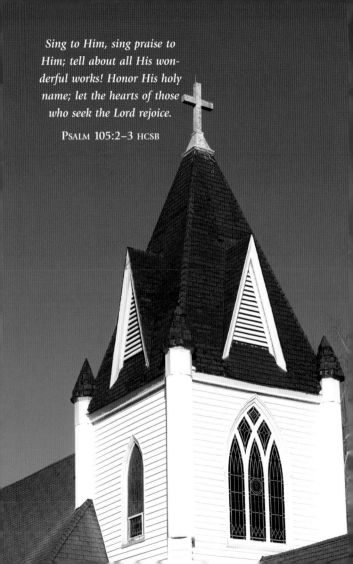

Sing to Him, sing praise to Him; tell about all His wonderful works! Honor His holy name; let the hearts of those who seek the Lord rejoice.

PSALM 105:2–3 HCSB

TRUST TAKES TIME

*Then they believed his words were true and
broke out in songs of praise.*
PSALM 106:12 MSG

It's profoundly freeing when you realize, "God, I
never want to be without you. I know you'll always
love and help me." It takes time to internalize that
God will never lie to you. It requires many instances

 of experiencing his faithful-
ness to completely under-
stand that God is absolutely
unlike the people who've
let you down.

Friend, truly trusting
God is never automatic,
but he's a patient and wise
teacher. So set your heart on realizing the truth about
him, and rejoice as you discover your best hopes are
true. Undoubtedly, when you learn to trust him and
see his faithful activity in your life, you'll want to
sing and shout for joy.

*God, "I never want to be without you. I know you'll
always love and help me." Please make this
prayer absolutely true in me. AMEN.*

*O L*ORD*, in Your favor toward Your
people; visit me with Your salvation,
that I may see the prosperity of Your
chosen ones, that I may rejoice in the
gladness of Your nation.*

P*SALM* 106:4–5 NASB

HIS HEALING WORD

He sent His word and healed them,
and delivered them from their destructions.
PSALM 107:20 NASB

The heart is a strange thing—it seems like nothing can heal it and there are no words for the depth of it.

Yet when you read the Bible, somehow your heart  is always helped. You continually find messages of encouragement that your heart drinks in like a desert traveler gulps down water. So why is God's Word different from other things you read?

Friend, through the Bible, God not only speaks to your mind, but also to your heart, soul, and spirit. His truth heals you.

Yes, the Bible is different from other reading materials because it's a balm to your spirit. So take a healthy dose—you'll feel better in no time.

God, grow my love for your Word and heal me with
it. Thank you for speaking to my mind, heart, soul,
and spirit with your truth. AMEN.

They cried to the LORD in their trouble,
and he saved them from their distress. He
brought them out of darkness and the
deepest gloom and broke away their chains.

PSALM 107:13–14 NIV

CALM

*He hushes the storm to a calm and to a gentle
whisper, so that the waves of the sea are still.*
PSALM 107:29 AMP

Your heart roars wildly in your chest, like a flag
flapping violently on a turbulent day. Chaos surrounds you. There's no time to think—just react to
the tornado of troubles that hit.

There's only one to cling
to because only God can
quiet this tumultuous mael-
strom.

So friend, pray. Repeat to
yourself the things you
know: God loves you and
can handle this situation. God is in control and will
help you. He's never let you down and never will.

The tempest may not pass immediately, but he'll
infuse you with his wonderful peace and empower
you with his strength. Then you'll know what it is to
have calm in the midst of the storm.

*God, I need your calming voice in my troubles. Please
help me. I will praise you because you give
me your peace and strength.* AMEN.

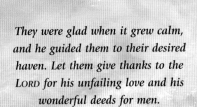

They were glad when it grew calm,
and he guided them to their desired
haven. Let them give thanks to the
LORD for his unfailing love and his
wonderful deeds for men.

PSALM 107:30–31 NIV

YOU CANNOT IMAGINE

Your love reaches higher than the heavens,
and your loyalty extends beyond the clouds.
PSALM 108:4 CEV

Think of the person you love most—the person you'd do anything for. Examine the depth of your love for him or her. Do you love that person more than yourself? Perhaps the one you love deepest is you.

Please understand that any love you could feel for another—or even for yourself—pales in comparison to the love of God. There's a limit to your love, but God's is unlimited. There are conditions to your love, but God's is unconditional. God's love is so vast, noble, and astounding that it's on a whole different level.

You cannot imagine how amazingly powerful and profound God's love is for you. So then rejoice that nothing can ever separate you from it.

God, I can't figure out or measure your love, but I
can thank you for it. Help me to trust
the height and depth of it. AMEN.

Answer us and save us by your power
so the people you love will be rescued.

PSALM 108:6 NCV

Respect and Obey

*Respect and obey the LORD! This is the
first step to wisdom and good sense.
God will always be respected.*

PSALM 111:10 CEV

OTHER PEOPLE'S FAILINGS

In return for my love they accuse me,
but I continue to pray.
PSALM 109:4 HCSB

Whenever someone hurts you, you can choose to take one of two paths. The first is the road of bitterness. You ruminate on their wounding words and 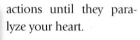 actions until they paralyze your heart.

The second is the road of blessing. This option leads you to God, to whom you release their cruelty against you. You realize that God has forgiven you of the wrongs you've done, and to be like him you must forgive them. This path brings you closer to God and develops his character within you.

People's failings can either draw you closer to God or paralyze your heart against him and others. Friend, you know the better path—so take it.

God, I've been harboring unforgiveness in my heart.
Please forgive me and help me forgive those who've
harmed me. Thank you for your love. AMEN.

I will give repeated thanks
to the LORD, praising him
to everyone. For he stands
beside the needy, ready to
save them from those who
condemn them.

PSALM 109:30–31 NLT

A PRIEST TO YOU ALWAYS

The Lord made a solemn promise and will not take it back: "You will be a priest forever."
Psalm 110:4 GNT

In the Old Testament, a priest would represent the people before God, teach them about him, and offer sacrifices for their sins. Unfortunately, earthly priests

were restricted in what they could do, and their sacrifices were only temporary.

Yet Psalm 110 speaks of the great High Priest who isn't limited in saving his people—that's Jesus. When Jesus came, he not only became the flawless, everlasting sacrifice for your offenses, he became your eternal High Priest. He constantly teaches you about God, and he prepares you to be close to God.

Jesus is your High Priest forever, and he's ideal for the job. Trust him with your deepest needs because he'll always represent you perfectly.

Jesus, thank you for being my High Priest—for reconciling me to God and forgiving me of my offenses. Truly, you are worthy of praise! Amen.

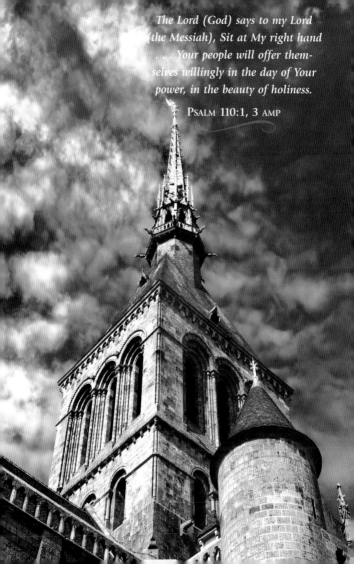

The Lord (God) says to my Lord
(the Messiah), Sit at My right hand
. . . Your people will offer themselves willingly in the day of Your
power, in the beauty of holiness.

PSALM 110:1, 3 AMP

TO BE WISE

Respect and obey the LORD! This is the first step to wisdom and good sense. God will always be respected.
PSALM 111:10 CEV

There are some people who are quite scholarly—they read all of the most prestigious journals and can thoroughly bewilder you with their lofty words and theories.

They seem to know everything. However, for all their knowledge, they don't always act in the wisest ways.

Yet there's great wisdom in this psalm, which declares we are to respect and obey God. After all, he really does know everything and never steers you wrong.

The basis of wisdom is to realize you don't know it all, but you do know the One who does. So to be wise, follow him. In the end, all the other sources of knowledge will pass away, but he will remain.

God, I don't know it all, but I'm thankful that you do. Help me to respect and obey you so I can have true wisdom. AMEN.

I will praise the LORD with my whole heart, in the assembly of the upright and in the congregation. The works of the LORD are great, studied by all who have pleasure in them.

PSALM 111:1–2 NKJV

LIGHT ALWAYS COMES

Even in darkness light dawns for the upright, for the gracious and compassionate and righteous man.
PSALM 112:4 NIV

There's fear in the unknown: how you'll pay your bills or reconcile that relationship; whether or not you'll recover from this illness or overcome that  obstacle. As if darkness covers your view, you cannot see what's ahead—or why this is happening to you.

Yet when you look to God, he sheds light on your situation. He'll not only give you assurance of his help, but more important, he'll show you the good that can come from your difficulties if you'll only focus on him.

Friend, no matter how dark and confusing your situation, God can illuminate it. So trust in him with all your heart and you'll be sure to see the light.

God, I need wisdom and understanding in this dark situation. Thank you for shedding light on it and showing me the good that'll come of it. AMEN.

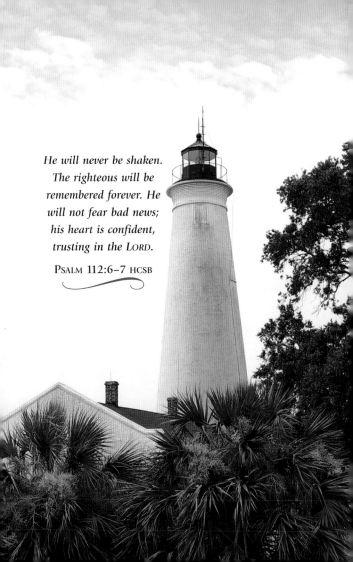

He will never be shaken.
The righteous will be
remembered forever. He
will not fear bad news;
his heart is confident,
trusting in the Lord.

Psalm 112:6–7 hcsb

NOT PERMANENT

He raises the poor from the dust; he lifts the needy from their misery and makes them companions of princes.
PSALM 113:7–8 GNT

One of the worst things about a hopeless situation is just that—it lacks any hope. You can't see any evidence that things will ever get better. The same difficulty  dogs you incessantly, wearing you down without any apparent possibility of reprieve.

Friend, the worst thing you can do is to assume your bad situation will never change—that it's beyond God's reach to improve. Yet your life can be transformed in an instant. From one moment to the next, God can lift you out of your bad circumstances.

Your situation is not permanent, but the love and grace of God is! So follow him. And praise God that he's going to transform your life for good.

God, thank you that this situation will not last forever, but your goodness to me does. I praise you for being my hope in every situation. AMEN.

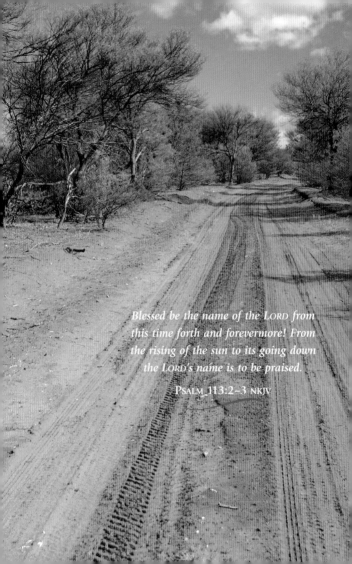

Blessed be the name of the LORD from
this time forth and forevermore! From
the rising of the sun to its going down
the LORD's name is to be praised.

PSALM 113:2–3 NKJV

ROCK TO WATER

He turned the rock into pools of water; yes,
springs of water came from solid rock.
PSALM 114:8 NLT

As the Israelites fled from Egypt across the desert, they were weary and parched—yet there was no water to quench their thirst. So Moses prayed, and God instructed him to strike a particular rock with

his staff. Moses obeyed the strange command, and the water flowed out.

This unimaginable miracle is your encouragement today: Whatever you yearn for, don't despair when you don't see it. God will use unexpected things in your path to provide

for your needs. Your responsibility is to obey his commands and trust his promises.

It'll take faith, friend, but God will help you. So do as he says. He'll transform your situation in a way you could never have dreamed.

God, thank you for the reminder that you can do
miracles in my situation. Lead me, and I'll follow.
Thank you for your love and power. AMEN.

Tremble, O earth, at the presence of the Lord.

PSALM 114:7 ESV

REAL AUTHORITY

Our God is in heaven; He does
whatever He pleases.
PSALM 115:3 NKJV

It's common to look up to those who are famous
and wealthy and imitate how they behave in order to
achieve what they have. Yet when you do so, you're

allowing them to influence
you. Do they really deserve
that power?

The truth is that only God
rightfully warrants that kind
of authority in your life.
When you focus on him and
consider what behavior
would please him, you're acting wisely. By studying
his Word, praying for wisdom, and considering his
viewpoint, you set yourself on the path to real success.

Friend, always seek God and make choices that
honor him. He is the only One who's truly worthy of
a say in your life.

God, please help me to understand how you would
handle my situation. Please reveal yourself to
me so that I can act like you. AMEN.

Trust in the LORD, all you that worship him. He helps you and protects you. The LORD remembers us . . . He will bless everyone who honors him, the great and the small alike.

PSALM 115:11–13 GNT

LIVE!

You have delivered my soul from death, my eyes from tears, and my feet from falling. I will walk before the Lord in the land of the living.
PSALM 116:8–9 NKJV

Are you a procrastinator? Do you get things done at the last minute? Friend, there's no procrastination for living—you either live or

you don't. If you're hiding from life out of fear of what will happen, you'll never live at all.

Yet God created you to have the abundant life. He wants you to be full of joy, and there's no better way to do that than loving and serving him with your whole heart, mind, soul, and strength.

It's understandable that you don't want to be hurt or rejected, but realize that you'll never lose God's love. So step out in faith—take the leap God's calling you to. Your abundant life awaits.

God, I don't want to procrastinate anymore. Please calm my fears, show me how to really live, and teach me how to serve you well. AMEN.

*O Lord, truly I am Your
servant. . . . You have loosed my
bonds. I will offer to You the
sacrifice of thanksgiving and will
call on the name of the Lord.*

PSALM 116:16–17 AMP

LOVE THAT COVERS THE WORLD

*Praise the LORD, all you nations. Praise him,
all you people of the earth.*
PSALM 117:1 NLT

Praise God that he loves all the people of the world. Exalt him because he cares for the young and the old, the poor and the wealthy, the weak and the strong, the helpless and the powerful.

 Every person, adore him—whether you're red, yellow, black, brown, or white; whether you're in Europe, Africa, Asia, Australia, or the Americas. In every language and dialect—from every urban, suburban, and rural house, apartment, farm, and hut—worship the Lord God Almighty!

He loves and accepts us all and waits for us to receive him by faith. So rejoice in him and let songs of praise cover the earth. Hallelujah! He loves us! Glory to his name!

God, the scope of your love is so deep, so wide, so great, so powerful, so all-encompassing! How faithful you are! Glory to your name! AMEN.

*Great is His faithful love to us;
the Lord's faithfulness endures
forever. Hallelujah!*

PSALM 117:2 HCSB

STEADFAST PROMISES

*It is better to trust in the LORD
than to depend on people.*
PSALM 118:8 GNT

What is it that you're waiting for today? Perhaps you've been disillusioned by people who've pledged to help you but have  failed to carry through. They may have even tried their best for you, but you're left disheartened all the same.

Friend, if God has given you a promise, then look to him to deliver it—he won't go back on his word. The people around you just don't have his power, wisdom, and creativity. Though they want to help you, they can never do so as perfectly as God can.

So trust God's promise to you and don't despair if you have to wait for it. Know that it's absolutely assured, and rejoice!

God, it's easier to have faith in someone I can see than in someone I can't. Please help me to trust your steadfast promises. AMEN.

The LORD is my
strength and my song;
he has given me victory.
Songs of joy and victory
are sung in the camp
of the godly. The
strong right arm of
the LORD has done
glorious things!

PSALM 118:14–15 NLT

ABSOLUTES

I have chosen the way of truth;
Your judgments I have laid before me.
PSALM 119:30 NKJV

As you get to know God and learn to love him more, he'll teach you the truth that sets you free. Though you're liberated immediately from sin by believing in him, he must continue to unshackle you

 from the harmful attitudes that have been deeply ingrained within you.

You must learn that there's one absolute reality—and it's based on God. This doesn't happen overnight. Rather, it's the passionate pursuit of a life dedicated to him. And every day, God is working toward that goal—setting you increasingly free by the truth he reveals to you.

So stick close to God and rejoice in the liberty you're gaining today. He will make you truly free, indeed!

God, you know the destructive attitudes that continue to hinder me. Thank you for teaching me the truth that heals and liberates me from them. AMEN.

I run in the path of your commands,
for you have set my heart free. Teach
me, O LORD, to follow your decrees;
then I will keep them to the end.

PSALM 119:32–33 NIV

ENCOURAGING OTHERS' SOULS

May those who fear You see me and be glad,
because I wait for Your word.
PSALM 119:74 NASB

Today you'll utilize talents that will benefit your
work and life. Those have been given to you for your
own survival and improvement.

Yet you also have spiritual gifts that are specifically
entrusted to you for the
sake of others. God imparted
those gifts so you could be
his instrument of blessing
and encouragement to those in need. Whether you
help, give, teach, pray, or serve, you represent God's
comfort and provision to them.

Friend, understand that you've been given the
wonderful privilege of showing God's love to all the
people who cross your path. So use your God-given
gifts for his glory! Others will undoubtedly be
encouraged and glad to have you around.

God, how would you have me encourage others
today? Please empower me to bless those around me
mightily with my spiritual gifts! AMEN.

Let your steadfast love comfort me
according to your promise to your servant. Let your mercy come to me, that
I may live; for your law is my delight.

PSALM 119:76–77 ESV

UNDERSTOOD BY THE SPIRIT

*The unfolding of your words gives light; it
imparts understanding to the simple.*
PSALM 119:130 ESV

Some call it the "Aha!" moment. You study a principle and still don't comprehend it. Then, one day, in
the midst of common activities, you suddenly get it.
"Aha!"

This happens many times with
spiritual concepts because God's
principles are not only learned by
your intellect, but also by your
willing spirit. We think of God's
truth as lofty and ethereal, but in
reality, his precepts must be understood in a practical way. You must be able to live them out from deep
within.

Friend, the God who is able to save your soul is
able to instruct you in his ways. So listen and learn
from him. He'll undoubtedly lead you to many profound "Aha!" moments.

*God, thank you for teaching your wisdom to my
spirit. Teach me your truth so that I can always
follow you well and praise you. AMEN.*

Your promise has been tested through and through, and I, your servant, love it dearly . . . The way you tell me to live is always right; help me understand it so I can live to the fullest.

PSALM 119:140, 144 MSG

WHAT'S WRONG HERE?

*Deliver me, O Lord, from lying lips
and from deceitful tongues.*
PSALM 120:2 AMP

As you're talking to someone, you feel it—like a sudden pause in your spirit. Something with what they're saying makes you feel uneasy, though it all appears right. What's going on?

Sometimes when you feel a hesitation about others, God may be cautioning you about their true intentions. Old-time believers called that a "check in the spirit." It's a divine signal that alerts you concerning some danger or deceit.

Friend, don't disregard God's warning, no matter how attractive or convincing the person. Pay attention to the "checks." Step back from the situation and watch it unfold. Certainly, God will show you what he's protected you from, and you'll be glad you listened to him.

God, thank you for warning me about the things that can harm me. Help me to heed your warnings and pay attention to the "checks." AMEN.

In my distress I cried to the Lord,
and He answered me.
PSALM 120:1 AMP

Our Help

Our help is in the name
of the LORD, who made
heaven and earth.

PSALM 124:8 NKJV

SLEEP WELL

*The LORD is your protector, and he won't
go to sleep or let you stumble.*
PSALM 121:3 CEV

Anxious about tomorrow? Are your concerns keeping you awake? Fears can rob you of the rest you know you need and make you even weaker.

Yet you can sleep peacefully knowing that God is guarding you. So turn your thoughts and prayers to him. Remember that your help comes from him and that he's with you no matter what you'll face. He will give you wisdom for your situation and keep you from harm.

Though you're concerned for what will develop as you slumber, understand that God is watching the situation closely. He is your guard—observing what you cannot and preparing you for what's ahead. So remember your Protector and sleep well.

*God, thank you for protecting me while I sleep. Please
help me turn my concerns over to you, knowing
you'll help me in every situation. AMEN.*

*The Lord will protect you
and keep you safe from
all dangers. The Lord will
protect you now and
always wherever you go.*

PSALM 121:7–8 CEV

LIKE-MINDED

I rejoiced with those who said to me,
"Let us go to the house of the LORD."
PSALM 122:1 HCSB

Do your friends love God and teach you about his goodness? Do they encourage you to know him better through Bible study and prayer? Do they help you make godly decisions?

Your friends will either bring you closer to God, or they'll make it harder for you to remain faithful to him. That's not to say you should abandon the friends that don't know God, but you must be careful about how they influence you—and how you inspire them.

It's wise to spend time with people who also love God—so seek out and befriend those who serve him. They'll undoubtedly bless you and help you grow in your relationship with him.

God, thank you for my godly friends. Please
help me befriend more people who honor
you and will help me grow closer to you. AMEN.

For my brothers and companions' sake
I will say, "Peace be within you!"

PSALM 122:8 ESV

IT'S WHAT YOU LOOK TO

*I lift my eyes to You, the One
enthroned in heaven.*
PSALM 123:1 HCSB

Whatever fills your eyes will permeate your thoughts and ultimately affect your behavior. Continually view destructive content, and eventually you'll either be likewise aggressive in your dealings with others, or too afraid to venture out.

Yet if your focus is continually on God, you'll resemble him more and have increasing confidence in his power and goodness. That's why it's so important to concentrate your attention on God and pray to him continually—because he strengthens your soul.

Friend, what do you set your focus on? Consider it carefully because it'll affect you profoundly. So lift your gaze to the One enthroned in heaven, and fill your eyes and heart with the only One truly worthwhile.

*God, I want you to fill my eyes, permeate my
thoughts, and change my behavior to be like you. I
will focus on you, God—now and always.* AMEN.

We will keep looking to you,
O LORD *our God.*

PSALM 123:2 GNT

HIS NAME IS OUR HELP

*Our help is in the name of the LORD,
who made heaven and earth.*
PSALM 124:8 NKJV

What sort of help do you need today? Call upon God. He is:

The Great I am—The God who is the same yesterday, today, and forever. As he's helped others in the past, he'll help you.

El Shaddai—The Almighty God who defends you against every enemy or evil.

Yahweh Rapha—The God who heals all of your wounds.

Yahweh Yireh—He's your provider who cares for all of your needs.

Yahweh Shalom—He himself is your peace.

Yahweh M'Kaddesh—He's the one who makes you ready for salvation.

So call upon your wonderful God! He loves you greatly and he's always ready to help you, no matter what you need.

God, your flawless character and wonderful name always perfectly provide for all my needs. Your name is above every other, and I praise you forever! AMEN.

Oh, blessed be God! He didn't go off and leave us. He didn't abandon us defenseless.

PSALM 124:6 MSG

A MOUNTAIN UNSHAKABLE

Those who trust in God are like Zion Mountain: nothing can move it, a rock-solid mountain you can always depend on.
PSALM 125:1 MSG

Tragedy strikes, but you have to be strong. The wind is knocked out of you, but you must stay steady for others. You try to be brave, but you just want to cry.

Friend, the more you insist you're an unshakable mountain of strength, the more likely you are to crumble.

If you really want to be strong for those around you, then direct them to God and be honest about how he helps you in your weakness. It's your trust in God that makes you strong, not anything you can do on your own. So go ahead and weep, but also trust God to be strong enough for you—and everyone else as well.

God, thank you that I don't have to be the strong one, because you're strong enough for all of us. Thank you for your great comfort. AMEN.

As the mountains surround Jerusalem,
the Lord surrounds his people now
and forever.

PSALM 125:2 NCV

TEARDROPS

They who sow in tears shall
reap in joy and singing.
PSALM 126:5 AMP

God has not allowed one of your tears to drop to
the ground—he's caught them all and made them
into something beautiful. By all that you've been
through, you've been uniquely trained to comfort

those who are going through the
same thing.

You know what it is to hurt as
they hurt, fear as they fear, and
yearn as they yearn. You can
show them how to survive and
be comforted as you have been
comforted.

The tears of your biggest hurts have been resound-
ingly transformed into your most amazing opportunities for ministry. So today praise God for helping
you overcome your trials and console others with
the wisdom you have received.

God, I praise you for turning my biggest defeats into
my greatest victories. Thank you for your marvelous
comfort—help me to share it with others. AMEN.

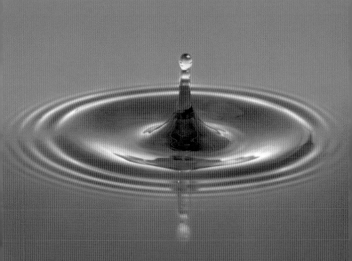

*He who goes out weeping, carrying seed
to sow, will return with songs of joy.*

PSALM 126:6 NIV

USELESS?

*Unless the L*ORD* builds a house, its builders labor over it in vain; unless the L*ORD* watches over a city, the watchman stays alert in vain.*
PSALM 127:1 HCSB

Solomon is known as the wisest man who ever lived, and he knew one thing to be absolutely true: Everything must have God at its foundation. Success,

security, and joy all must be established through God's wisdom and power or they will fade away.

This is because anything that's not based on God returns to dust. Yet everything that God does lasts forever.

Friend, you're working hard for what you have, but if God isn't leading you, you're chasing the wind. So spend your life on things that will have everlasting results. Obey God and trust his superb plans for you—because when you work for him, you know it's never in vain.

*God, I don't want to waste my life working for things that won't last. Please lead me and help me do whatever you ask. A*MEN.

It is useless to work so hard for a living, getting up early and going to bed late. For the LORD provides for those he loves, while they are asleep.

PSALM 127:2 GNT

RETURN FOR THE WORK

You shall eat the fruit of the labor of your hands;
you shall be blessed, and it shall be well with you.
PSALM 128:2 ESV

There's unacknowledged work that you do faithfully—at home, in your vocation, and in the community—because you want to honor God. It may not be glamorous or fun work—in fact, it's most

likely humble and monotonous—but you do your best at it because you know it's right.

Friend, that work isn't for nothing. Though you may not see any fruit from your labor right now, the seeds of your loyal service are taking root and will soon produce wonderful results.

So continue being an exceptional family member, co-worker, mentor, and friend because your faithfulness is making a big difference in the lives of others. And be patient, because what will bloom is going to bless you.

God, thank you for rewarding the work I do every day
for my loved ones, friends, and co-workers. Though
they may not see it, you always bless me. Amen.

A man who obeys the LORD
will surely be blessed.

PSALM 128:4 GNT

FROM CHILDHOOD

They have greatly oppressed me from my youth, but they have not gained the victory over me.
PSALM 129:2 NIV

There are issues that have plagued you since you were young. Perhaps they developed because of how you were raised or because of your own insecurities, and maybe they've resulted in a poor self-image or  the incorrect belief that somehow you're unlovable.

If so, these issues will crop back up when you're under pressure and cause you to doubt yourself and God. Yet they're not too difficult for God to overcome—he'll assuredly heal you from them and give you the victory.

Friend, whatever you've been struggling with can be conquered through God's power—so don't be afraid of those issues anymore. Claim the triumph over them and know that God makes you loveable, whole, and completely acceptable.

God, thank you that I don't have to live under the oppression of these issues any longer. Thank you for freeing and loving me, Lord God. AMEN.

The Lord is [uncompromisingly] righteous;
He has cut asunder the thick cords by
which the wicked [enslaved us].

PSALM 129:4 AMP

WHY FEAR THE FORGIVER?

There is forgiveness with You,
that You may be feared.
PSALM 130:4 NASB

It seems like a paradox: God loves you and forgives your sins, but you're still supposed to fear him. Why should you dread someone who pardons you?

Though fear and forgiveness seem like contradictory concepts, they actually go hand-in-hand. That's because godly fear is not terror; it's reverence.

When you truly respect God, you honor his commands. You also acknowledge when you violate his law because you want to maintain a good relationship with him.

Out of reverence to God, you confess your sins; out of love, he heals and pardons you. So ultimately, fear and forgiveness teach you the love of the Lord—and that, dear friend, is a very good thing.

God, thank you for teaching me about your healing
and forgiveness. I don't want to sin against you; I
want to have loving reverence for you. AMEN.

With all my heart, I am waiting, Lord,
for you! I trust your promises . . . Trust
the LORD! He is always merciful, and
he has the power to save you.

PSALM 130:5, 7 CEV

STOP COMPETING

God, I'm not trying to rule the roost, I don't want to be king of the mountain. I haven't meddled where I have no business.
PSALM 131:1 MSG

Who is it that gets under your skin? You can't stand to see them achieve anything because you're convinced they don't deserve success as much as you

do. When they do well, you're devastated.

You're struggling from a toxic mix of jealousy and pride—and no good can come of it. Even if that person is really as rotten as you believe, you're only hurting

yourself by harboring such bitter thoughts.

Friend, life isn't about competing with others, but about the purpose God has for you—and nobody can keep you from that except you. So stop competing and start praying for those people. God will change them through your prayers—and will certainly transform you as well!

God, please forgive me for being so negative about others. Teach me how to pray for them so that they'll know your love and salvation. AMEN.

*Hope in the LORD from this
time forth and forever.*

PSALM 131:3 NKJV

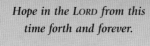

THE PROMISED
ANOINTED ONE

My anointed one will be a light for my people.
PSALM 132:17 NLT

The Ark of the Covenant was important to Israel
because God's presence would shine above it once a
year on the Day of Atonement. Psalm 132 was written to commemorate the day
when the Ark was brought back
to Jerusalem after a long time
away. Yet it also looked forward
to the day when God's presence
would constantly shine on his
people.

Friend, that day came when
the anointed one—Jesus—came as the Light of the
World. Because of him, you can constantly have
God's presence in your life—every minute of every
day. So embrace God's light by believing in Jesus,
and thank him that you never have to live in darkness again.

*Jesus, I do believe in you! Thank you for opening
the way to God for me, and for constantly
shining his light on my life. AMEN.*

"Here I will dwell, for I have desired it.
I will abundantly bless her provision . . .
I will clothe with salvation, and her
godly ones will sing aloud for joy."

PSALM 132:14–16 NASB

UNIFIED

How good and how pleasant it is for
brethren to dwell together in unity!
PSALM 133:1 NKJV

In the human body, muscles, bones, and tendons; glands and nerves; and the cardiovascular, digestive, immune, and respiratory systems all coordinate to comprise a living being. Though they are different in

their functions, they all work together to keep you going.

Your body is truly amazing—and it's the perfect way to understand how we relate to each other as God's people. God doesn't want us to be exactly alike—he created us with special talents and unique strengths. Yet we all come together for the extraordinary purpose of serving him.

Love for God is the basis of our unity—not conformity. So serve God with your whole heart and you're sure to fit right in.

God, thank you for creating me with a unique purpose that fits right in with your people. I praise you for uniting us all in love. AMEN.

The Lord has promised to bless his people with life forevermore.

Psalm 133:3 cev

A REASON TO LIVE FOREVER

Come, praise the LORD, all his servants,
all who serve in his Temple.
PSALM 134:1 GNT

Forever—that's a really long time. In fact, eternity is so overwhelming, many may wonder what we'll be doing. Other than eating at God's banquet and worshiping at his throne, won't we get bored?

But heaven isn't just puffy clouds and flowing robes. Whatever your purpose is on earth, it'll be even more joyous and fulfilling in eternity— because there, you won't face any of the hindrances that you have here. Rather, you'll praise God in creative ways you've never dreamed of.

Friend, don't underestimate the overpowering awe of being in the magnificent presence of your Creator. He's more wonderful than you ever hoped. You're going to love heaven—and it's certain you'll never want to leave.

God, I don't know what we'll be doing in heaven, but as long as I'm in your presence, I'll have everything I need. Hallelujah and amen!

Lift your praising hands to the Holy Place,
and bless GOD. In turn, may God of
Zion bless you—GOD who made
heaven and earth!

Psalm 134:2–3 MSG

Dwell in Unity

How good and how pleasant it is for brethren to dwell together in unity!

PSALM 133:1 NKJV

DESTRUCTIBLE VERSUS ETERNAL

The idols of the nations are of silver and gold,
made by human hands. They have mouths,
but cannot speak, eyes, but cannot see.
PSALM 135:15–16 HCSB

When the people of Israel got impatient for God to act, they'd mold an idol and ask it for help. Of course, these lifeless statuettes couldn't hear, speak,

or move—they were useless. But the Israelites wanted something they could put their hands on to trust.

The same is true when you base your security on your job, wealth, or some other tangible thing. You're trusting in something constructed with human hands that can also be destroyed by human hands. True, you cannot see God, but you're assured that your faith in him is well-founded because he is faithful and everlasting.

Friend, don't give up hope; keep believing in God. He'll never disappoint you.

God, sometimes I wish I had something tangible to
put my trust in, but I know you're the only
One truly worthy of my faith. AMEN.

Your name, O LORD, endures forever;
your fame, O LORD, is known to
every generation. For the LORD will
vindicate his people and have
compassion on his servants.

PSALM 135:13–14 NLT

EXPRESSING YOUR GRATITUDE

Give thanks to the Lord of lords. His love continues forever. Only he can do great miracles.
PSALM 136:3–4 NCV

It's customary to seek God when you're hurting and need his intervention—but how often do you simply communicate your thankfulness to him?

Friend, you should show appreciation to God in every situation because it helps you rightly refocus your attention on him. Articulating your gratefulness strengthens your love for him and also refreshes your soul.

So stop what you're doing right now and praise God. Express your gratefulness to him for all the loving ways he's provided for you. Thank him for the good he's bringing out of your most difficult situations and the blessings he's creating that you cannot yet see. Then just worship him for who he is.

Feels wonderful, doesn't it?

God, it does feel fantastic to thank you and worship you for your loving-kindness to me. You are utterly amazing and worthy of all my gratefulness! AMEN.

O give thanks to the God of heaven, for His mercy and loving-kindness endure forever!

PSALM 136:26 AMP

REMEMBERING THE DREAM

*May my tongue cling to the roof of my mouth if
I do not remember you, if I do not consider
Jerusalem my highest joy.*
PSALM 137:6 NIV

When God's people went into captivity in
Babylon, they kept their hopes up by remembering
their capital city of Jerusalem. Thoughts of returning

to Jerusalem motivated them to
persevere and not succumb to
despair.

Friend, when you lose sight of
your dreams, your life can
become drudgery. In fact, if
you're struggling today, you may
have forgotten the vision God
has given you. Yet you should
never get so discouraged by your circumstances that
you disregard his promises.

Whenever you lose your passion for life, realize it's
either because you've stopped pursuing your dreams
or because you've forgotten that it's God who
empowers you to achieve them. So today get back on
track by remembering.

*God, thank you for reminding me of your promises
and reenergizing my life. May I never forget the great
dreams you're fulfilling in me. AMEN.*

May I never be able to play the harp again if I forget you, Jerusalem!

PSALM 137:5 GNT

FULFILLING AND FULFILLED

The LORD will fulfill his purpose for me; your love, O LORD, endures forever—do not abandon the works of your hands.
PSALM 138:8 NIV

As you learn about God's purpose for your life, don't be surprised if others don't comprehend the course he's taking.

Many people didn't understand why God would make an insignificant shepherd boy like David king over Israel. They were also confounded about why David wasn't more proactive about seizing the throne from King Saul. Yet David ignored the others and trusted God's plan—and God blessed him for it.

The same is true when others doubt you or insist you take a particular course of action. Remember that your responsibility is to obey God and learn from him. You can always trust that he is accomplishing his promises in the best way possible for you.

God, thank you for fulfilling your plans in the most instructive and encouraging way for me. Help me always to obey you, Lord God. AMEN.

Thank you for your love, thank you for your faithfulness; most holy is your name, most holy is your Word. The moment I called out, you stepped in; you made my life large with strength.

PSALM 138:2–3 MSG

PROFOUND KNOWING

*O Lord, you have searched me
[thoroughly] and have known me.*
PSALM 139:1 AMP

You can keep up a front with other people—it's a way to protect yourself when you feel insecure. You conceal your flaws and fears so people can't hurt  you. Unfortunately, your defenses also stop you from receiving their love.

Yet you cannot hide from God. He knows you completely and is aware that those defenses are stopping you from having the life you were created for. That's why he chips away at them until you can fully experience his love.

Friend, God knows you more profoundly than you know yourself—and he's declared that you're worth loving. Therefore, let him tear down those defenses so that others can know and love you as well.

God, you're my Protector—not the defenses I've built up. Please tear down the harmful walls in my life so I can fully experience your love. AMEN.

Where could I go to escape from you? . . . If
I flew away beyond the east or lived in the
farthest place in the west, you would be there
to lead me, you would be there to help me.

PSALM 139:7, 9–10 GNT

YOU'RE MADE WELL

*I praise you because of the wonderful way
you created me. Everything you do is
marvelous! Of this I have no doubt.*
PSALM 139:14 CEV

What do you see when you look in the mirror? Do you see an imperfect facial feature or a waistline that needs adjustment?

Society generally puts a lot of emphasis on outward appearance, but there's so much more to attractiveness than mere looks. There's character and all of the attributes that God builds in you, such as love, joy, peace, patience, kindness, goodness, faithfulness, humility, and self-control.

Friend, God didn't make any mistakes or use any unworthy materials when he put you together. Rather, he skillfully created you with your own unique beauty and potential.

So whenever you're at the mirror, remember that you're God's work of art, and he's completely delighted with you.

*God, thank you for the way you created me. Please
help me to see the beauty and potential you
see in me and in others. AMEN.*

Nothing about me is hidden
from you! . . . With your own
eyes you saw my body being
formed. Even before
I was born, you had
written in your book
everything I
would do.

PSALM 139:15–16
CEV

THOUGHT-ATTACK

Lord GOD, my strong Savior, You shield
my head on the day of battle.
PSALM 140:7 HCSB

You've heard of psych-ops—the strategy of waging war within the mind and intimidating enemies by undermining what they believe.

That's essentially what happens in your spiritual life—your old, destructive thoughts battle against  God's truth and the good he's doing in you. God promises you success, but those thoughts predict failure. God says he loves and accepts you, but you only remember when others rejected you.

But God transforms your mind and cleanses it of negative thoughts when you study his Word. Whenever the bad thoughts return, you subdue them by repeating his promises.

That's why you should continually focus on God—because with him, eventually you'll be truly victorious on the battleground of your mind.

God, please help me to get rid of those negative and
untrue thoughts. Remind me of your Word so
that I can think triumphantly. AMEN.

Surely the righteous shall give thanks to Your name; the upright shall dwell in Your presence.

PSALM 140:13 NKJV

A TROUBLING TONGUE

*Set a guard, O L*ORD*, over my mouth; keep*
watch over the door of my lips.
PSALM 141:3 NKJV

Do you say, "I can't" or "God can"? Do you declare,
"I'm not strong enough" or "I can do anything
through him who strengthens me"? Do you proclaim,

"It's impossible" or "With God
everything is possible"?

Think about what you articu-
late—do you focus on your
weaknesses or God's power?

It's no wonder your speech is
negative when you're constantly
measuring your burdens against
your ability to handle them.
However, when you focus on God, you realize that
he can handle anything you face.

Friend, you can either talk yourself into defeat or
call upon God for the victory. So voice your praises
to God's amazing power and perfect wisdom. It's the
surest way to triumph!

God, I praise you! I will speak out my confidence in
your love, wisdom, and power, because you truly
*deserve it. Thank you for the victory. A*MEN*.*

God, come close. Come quickly!
Open your ears—it's my voice
you're hearing! Treat my prayer
as sweet incense rising; my raised
hands are my evening prayers.

PSALM 141:1–2 MSG

CONSTRUCTIVE REBUKES

If a good person punished me, that would be kind. If he corrected me, that would be like perfumed oil on my head.
PSALM 141:5 NCV

The person who talks too loud may not realize she has a hearing problem. The person who stands too  close when conversing with others may not realize that he's making people feel uncomfortable. You may not even realize that you have broccoli in your teeth after lunch unless a friend points it out to you.

At times, there will be things about you that you won't realize are amiss, counterproductive, and even destructive. These foibles are blind spots that are impeding your progress.

Thankfully, God wants you to succeed, so he reveals those issues to you. Listen to him when he rebukes you, because he wants you to reach your full potential.

God, thank you for revealing my weaknesses, sins, and blind spots. Thank you for loving me enough to help me be all that I can be. AMEN.

I look to you for help, O Sovereign LORD. You are my refuge.

PSALM 141:8 NLT

PERSONAL PRISONS

*Rescue me from this prison, so I can praise your
name. And when your people notice your wonderful kindness to me, they will rush to my side.*
PSALM 142:7 CEV

Your troubles surround you like an army—driving
you forward though you long to rest. You feel like
you have no choices—you tackle your day, trying to
survive all the things that
have to be done.

Personal prisons take many
shapes and sizes, but they're
limiting all the same. Perhaps
yours is due to illness or
finances; or maybe there's a
demanding relationship that
requires your continual attention and care.

Friend, your situation is difficult, but it won't last
forever. God will eventually set you free. But in the
meantime, allow him to be your freedom. Even if
your time and activities are restricted, your spirit
isn't. So focus on him and discover true liberty.

*God, I don't know how to be free with all I
have to do, but I know you can teach
me your liberty. Thank you.* AMEN.

Lord, I cry out to you. I say,
"You are my protection. You
are all I want in this life."

Psalm 142:5 NCV

DIRECTION

Teach me to do Your will, for You are my God;
let Your good Spirit lead me on level ground.
PSALM 143:10 NASB

There are times when God will give you ease in your journey—like a falcon effortlessly gliding over a forest with no concern for the problems below. These are the blessed moments when you truly believe anything's possible with God.

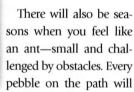

There will also be seasons when you feel like an ant—small and challenged by obstacles. Every pebble on the path will require an arduous climb, and it'll be difficult to make progress. These are also blessed moments because you'll learn to rely on God.

Whether simple or difficult, on the heights or in the depths—when God is directing you, you're always on stable, level ground. So proceed with confidence. He'll protect and teach you wherever you go.

God, whether easy or difficult, I'll follow wherever you
lead. Truly, you are perfect and wonderful. Thank you
for delighting in me and directing my path. AMEN.

Let me hear Your lovingkindness in the morning;
for I trust in You; teach me the way in which I
should walk; for to You I lift up my soul.

PSALM 143:8 NASB

TRAINED AND READY

*Blessed be the LORD, my rock, who trains my
hands for war, and my fingers for battle.*
PSALM 144:1 ESV

The obstacles in front of you will not defeat or
destroy you, but they will be the vessels by which
God brings you to your ultimate goal.

Recall David's battle against
Goliath and how all of Israel's
army was afraid to confront the
nine-foot Philistine giant. Even
the gargantuan Goliath could
not overcome David. David
gained the victory through
God's help, and eventually
Israel recognized David's leadership because of it.

Friend, do not fear your obstacles. Though you're
overwhelmed right now, you will not succumb to
them. Rather, thank God that he'll use them to fulfill
his promises to you. He's training you for a great victory, so face those obstacles with courage.

*God, thank you that these obstacles are really your
way of preparing me for your great promises to me.
I'll trust you through them all. AMEN.*

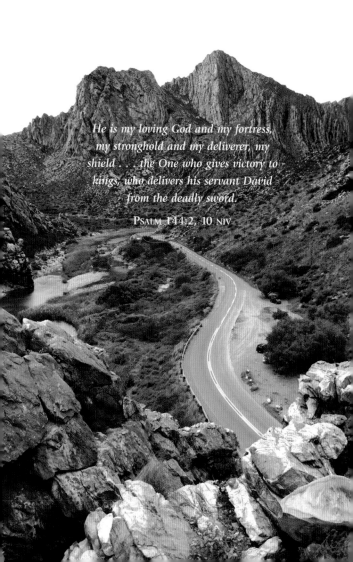

He is my loving God and my fortress,
my stronghold and my deliverer, my
shield . . . the One who gives victory to
kings, who delivers his servant David
from the deadly sword.

PSALM 144:2, 10 NIV

YOUR ATTENTION, PLEASE

*They will speak of the glory of Your kingdom and
will declare Your might, informing [all]
people of Your mighty acts.*
PSALM 145:11–12 HCSB

You have within your grasp the greatest message ever
known: There is one God who loves you and forgives
your sins. He saves you if you'll only believe in him.

Throughout history, the bravest,
most compassionate people have
proclaimed God's Word despite
persecution, pressure, and terrible
consequences. It was worth it
because the message is true—and
it transforms the life of whoever
accepts it.

You may be fearful of the attention God's message
will bring you, but understand that you're not
alone—you're part of an excellent history of people
who trusted God and told others about him.

So join the boundless throng of people who proclaim God's salvation. You're truly in great company!

*God, thank you for your saving Word and for all
who've proclaimed it. Thank you for teaching me the
greatest message ever known. AMEN.*

My mouth will declare the Lord's praise; let every living thing praise His holy name forever and ever.

Psalm 145:21 HCSB

SEEING GLORY CLEARLY

He judges in favor of the oppressed and gives
food to the hungry. The LORD sets prisoners free
and . . . lifts those who have fallen.
PSALM 146:7–8 GNT

It's true that you'll always have troubles, but can you imagine what you'd miss out on if you never experienced pain or challenges? Life would be extremely different, but it wouldn't necessarily be better.

That's because your trials, though difficult, teach you what's really important in life and how to console others suffering similar circumstances. Most important, your afflictions confirm that God is real—because through them, his profoundly deep, healing comfort transforms your soul.

Friend, if you never face an impossible situation, how could you ever see God's glory or experience the power of his presence? You couldn't. So thank God that even your troubles have a wonderful purpose when you see them through his love.

God, thank you that through my trials I can see your
glory. I praise you that even my suffering can become
a blessing through your healing touch. AMEN.

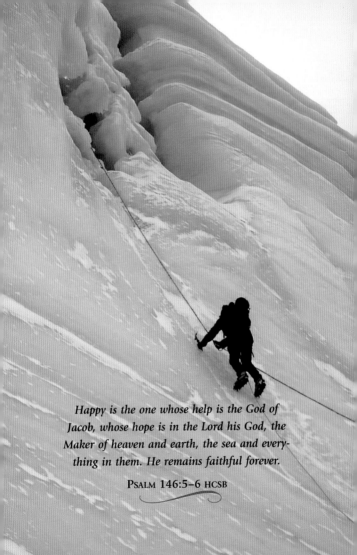

Happy is the one whose help is the God of Jacob, whose hope is in the Lord his God, the Maker of heaven and earth, the sea and everything in them. He remains faithful forever.

PSALM 146:5–6 HCSB

NO HIGHER FRIEND

He counts the stars and calls them all by name.
How great is our Lord! His power is absolute!
His understanding is beyond comprehension!
PSALM 147:4–5 NLT

Understand that there are things you cannot determine. No matter your wisdom or expertise, there's an entire universe of information that's completely  unknowable to the human mind. Science cannot measure heaven, and literature has yet to faintly imagine it.

Yet God comprehends it all, for it comes from his making. And he's also aware of each breath you take, every hair on your head, and all the cells in your body. No one has such a complete and lofty understanding as God does.

So ask yourself: Where can you go for counsel that is better than God's? You may be limited, but God isn't. Truly, he is your wisest and most wonderful Friend.

God, sometimes it's hard for me to remember that I
don't know everything, but you do. Teach me your
wisdom so I can walk in your ways. AMEN.

Sing to God a thanksgiving hymn, play music on your instruments to God, who fills the sky with clouds, preparing rain for the earth, then turning the mountains green.

PSALM 147:7–8 MSG

THE CREATION SPEAKS OF HIM

Praise him, you highest heavens, and you waters
above the heavens! Let them praise the name of the
LORD! For he commanded and they were created.
PSALM 148:4–5 ESV

Why does the psalmist tell the creation to praise God?
Do the heavens have a voice? Can the sun and moon
declare God's glory? In a sense, the answer is yes.

Consider the question this way:
When you go to a gallery, do you
commend the artwork or the
painter? When you eat a delicious
meal, do you extol the food or the
expertise of the chef? Is it the over-
ture or the composer that inspires
your awe?

The creation reflects the brilliance of the Creator—it
doesn't draw attention to itself.

Remember that the next time God works through
you to do something wonderful—and direct all the
glory, honor, and praise to him.

God, you are the source of everything lovely that
comes from me. May my life reflect your glory,
wisdom, and honor—and always bring you praise.
AMEN.

All creation, come praise the
name of the LORD. Praise his
name alone. The glory of God is
greater than heaven and earth.

PSALM 148:13 CEV

YOUR INSTRUMENT OF CHOICE

Praise the LORD! Sing to the LORD a new song . . .
Praise his name with dancing, accompanied
by tambourine and harp.
PSALM 149:1, 3 NLT

What's the right way to praise the Lord? Do you use a stringed instrument or a tambourine? Do you sing a beautiful melody or recite an eloquent speech? Do

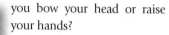

you bow your head or raise your hands?

First and foremost, praise to God must come from the heart—with an attitude of joy, honor, and love for him. After

that, your praise can express itself in countless ways.

David himself praised God on an instrument, with dancing, and through writing psalms. He didn't limit the creative ways he could express his adoration for God. Neither should you.

So exalt God in everything you do and with every-thing you've got. Truly, your loving God deserves it.

God, I praise you with all my heart, soul, mind,
strength, and talent. You are honorable and
worthy of all my love and thankfulness. AMEN.

The LORD takes delight in his people; he crowns the humble with salvation. Let the saints rejoice in this honor and sing for joy.

PSALM 149:4–5 NIV

WITH EVERY BREATH

Let every living, breathing creature
praise God! Hallelujah!
PSALM 150:6 MSG

In life, all things come to an end—except, of course, your relationship with God. That continues for all of eternity. When your circumstances seem hopeless, he

 shows you the victory. When everything else fails, his love remains steadfast.

That's why it's wonderful when you learn to walk with him and praise him with every breath you take. You're building the most important relationship—the one that lasts forever. You discover how to rely on him and trust him no matter what challenges may come.

Friend, today—and for all of your days—praise God with every breath and continue on in the blessing of his presence. For that truly is a life well spent.

God, thank you for never leaving me! Teach me to
praise you so that each day I will grow closer
to you and love you more. AMEN.

Praise the Lord! Praise God in His sanctuary;
praise Him in His mighty firmament!
Praise Him for His mighty acts; praise Him
according to His excellent greatness!

PSALM 150:1–2 NKJV

Hallelujah!